Changes in Sediment Volume in Alder Lake, Nisqually River Basin, Washington, 1945–2011

By Jonathan A. Czuba, Theresa D. Olsen, Christiana R. Czuba, Christopher S. Magirl, and Casey C. Gish

Prepared in cooperation with Pierce County Public Works and Utilities, Surface Water Management, and King County Department of Natural Resources and Parks, Water and Land Resources Division

Open-File Report 2012–1068

U.S. Department of the Interior
U.S. Geological Survey

U.S. Department of the Interior
KEN SALAZAR, Secretary

U.S. Geological Survey
Marcia K. McNutt, Director

U.S. Geological Survey, Reston, Virginia: 2012

For more information on the USGS—the Federal source for science about the Earth,its natural and living resources, natural hazards, and the environment—visit http://www.usgs.gov or call 1–888–ASK–USGS

For an overview of USGS information products, including maps, imagery, and publications,visit http://www.usgs.gov/pubprod

To order this and other USGS information products, visit http://store.usgs.gov

Suggested citation: Czuba, J.A., Olsen, T.D., Czuba, C.R., Magirl, C.S., and Gish, C.C., 2012, Changes in sediment volume in Alder Lake, Nisqually River Basin, Washington, 1945–2011: U.S. Geological Survey Open-File Report 2012–1068, 30 p.

Contents

Abstract...1

Introduction..1

    Purpose and Scope 3

Description of Nisqually River Basin...3

    Brief History of Dams on the Nisqually River..3

    Major Debris Flows from Mount Rainier in the Nisqually River Basin 5

Methods...6

    Description of Historical Contour Maps and Conversion to Digital Format................................6

        1945 Elevation-Contour Map...6

        1956 Elevation-Contour Map...6

        1985 Elevation-Contour Map...6

        Digital Conversion of Historical Contour Maps to Elevation Surfaces 6

    Data Collection and Processing of 2011 Bathymetric Survey.......................................7

    Computation of Change in Volume between Elevation Surfaces 8

Changes in Sediment Volume of the Nisqually River Delta in Alder Lake............................9

Changes in Sediment Volume of the Little Nisqually River Delta in Alder Lake...................22

Sediment Deposition in Alder Lake 1945–2011...26

Future Investigations...27

Summary..27

Acknowledgments..28

References Cited..28

Figures

Figure 1. Map showing location and extent of Alder Lake within the Nisqually River basin, Washington 2

Figure 2. Photograph showing construction of Alder Dam on the Nisqually River, Washington, July 20, 1943 4

Figure 3. Photograph showing Alder Dam on the Nisqually River, Washington 5

Figure 4. Map showing the 1945 (pre-dam) surface elevations of the Alder Lake area, Washington 9

Figure 5. Map showing the 2011 point-elevation data of the bed of Alder Lake, Washington 10

Figure 6. Graph showing elevation profiles along the pre-dam Nisqually River centerline for the 1945 (pre-dam) and 2011 surfaces of the bed of the Alder Lake, Washington 11

Figure 7. Maps showing surface elevations of the Nisqually River delta in Alder Lake, Washington, from 1945 (pre-dam; contours at 5-foot intervals); 1956 (contours at 1-foot intervals); 1985 (contours mostly at 10-foot intervals, with a few contours at 5-foot intervals); and 2011 12

Figure 8. Photograph showing sediment deposited in Alder Lake near Elbe, Washington, March 28, 1956 16

Figures—Continued

Figure 9. Graph showing elevation profiles for the 1945 (pre-dam), 1956, 1985, and 2011 surfaces along a line through the approximate center of the Nisqually River delta in Alder Lake, Washington 17

Figure 10. Maps showing net change in elevation of the Nisqually River delta in Alder Lake, Washington, for 1945–56, 1945–85, and 1945–2011 18

Figure 11. Photograph showing view looking south at the southeast bank of Alder Lake, Washington, near the center of the lake, April 19, 2011 21

Figure 12. Maps showing spatial extent of the surfaces used to compute delta volume for the Little Nisqually River delta in Alder Lake, Washington, from 1945 (pre-dam; contours at 5-foot intervals) and 2011 23

Figure 13. Graph showing elevation profiles along the pre-dam Little Nisqually River centerline from 1945 (pre-dam) and 2011 surfaces of the Little Nisqually River delta in Alder Lake, Washington 24

Figure 14. Map showing change in elevation of the Little Nisqually River delta in Alder Lake, Washington, 1945–2011 25

Figure 15. Map showing the volume of sediment deposition between 1945 and 2011 at three areas of Alder Lake, Washington: the Nisqually River delta; the main body of Alder Lake, along a 40-meter wide corridor of the pre-dam Nisqually River; and the Little Nisqually River delta 27

Tables

Table 1. Net cumulative change in sediment volume of the Nisqually River delta in Alder Lake, Washington, and estimated uncertainty, 1945–56, 1945–85, and 1945–2011 22

Table 2. Incremental net change in sediment volume of the Nisqually River delta in Alder Lake, Washington, 1945–56, 1956–85, and 1985–2011 22

Table 3. Net change in sediment volume of the Little Nisqually River delta in Alder Lake, Washington, and estimated uncertainty, 1945–2011 26

Conversion Factors, Datums, and Abbreviations and Acronyms

Conversion Factors

Inch/Pound to SI

Multiply	By	To obtain
Length		
foot (ft)	0.3048	meter (m)

SI to Inch/Pound

Multiply	By	To obtain
Length		
meter (m)	3.281	foot (ft)
kilometer (km)	0.6214	mile (mi)
meter (m)	1.094	yard (yd)
Area		
square kilometer (km^2)	247.1	acre
square kilometer (km^2)	0.3861	square mile (mi^2)
Volume		
cubic meter (m^3)	35.31	cubic foot (ft^3)
cubic meter (m^3)	1.308	cubic yard (yd^3)
Sediment yield		
cubic meter per year per square kilometer [(m^3/yr)/km^2]	0.0006844	million gallons per year per square mile [(Mgal/yr)/mi^2]

Temperature in degrees Celsius (°C) may be converted to degrees Fahrenheit (°F) as follows:

$$°F=(1.8×°C)+32.$$

Datums

Vertical coordinate information is referenced to the North American Vertical Datum of 1988 (NAVD 88).

Horizontal coordinate information is referenced to the North American Datum of 1983 (NAD 83).

Elevation, as used in this report, refers to distance above the vertical datum.

Abbreviations and Acronyms

Abbreviation or Acronym	Definition
ADCP	acoustic Doppler current profiler
DRG	digital raster graphic
GIS	geographic information system
GPS	global positioning system
NAIP	National Agriculture Imagery Program
RTK	real-time kinematic
UTM10	Universal Transverse Mercator zone 10
USGS	U.S. Geological Survey
WSDOT	Washington State Department of Transportation

Changes in Sediment Volume in Alder Lake, Nisqually River Basin, Washington, 1945–2011

By Jonathan A. Czuba, Theresa D. Olsen, Christiana R. Czuba, Christopher S. Magirl, and Casey C. Gish

Abstract

The Nisqually River drains the southwest slopes of Mount Rainier, a glaciated stratovolcano in the Cascade Range of western Washington. The Nisqually River was impounded behind Alder Dam when the dam was completed in 1945 and formed Alder Lake. This report quantifies the volume of sediment deposited by the Nisqually and Little Nisqually Rivers in their respective deltas in Alder Lake since 1945. Four digital elevation surfaces were generated from historical contour maps from 1945, 1956, and 1985, and a bathymetric survey from 2011. These surfaces were used to compute changes in sediment volume since 1945. Estimates of the volume of sediment deposited in Alder Lake between 1945 and 2011 were focused in three areas: (1) the Nisqually River delta, (2) the main body of Alder Lake, along a 40-meter wide corridor of the pre-dam Nisqually River, and (3) the Little Nisqually River delta. In each of these areas the net deposition over the 66-year period was 42,000,000 ± 4,000,000 cubic meters (m³), 2,000,000 ± 600,000 m³, and 310,000 ± 110,000 m³, respectively. These volumes correspond to annual rates of accumulation of 630,000 ± 60,000 m³/yr, 33,000 ± 9,000 m³/yr, and 4,700 ± 1,600 m³/yr, respectively. The annual sediment yield of the Nisqually (1,100 ± 100 cubic meters per year per square kilometer [(m³/yr)/km²]) and Little Nisqually River basins [70 ± 24 (m³/yr)/km²] provides insight into the yield of two basins with different land cover and geomorphic processes. These estimates suggest that a basin draining a glaciated stratovolcano yields approximately 15 times more sediment than a basin draining forested uplands in the Cascade Range. Given the cumulative net change in sediment volume in the Nisqually River delta in Alder Lake, the total capacity of Alder Lake since 1945 decreased about 3 percent by 1956, 8 percent by 1985, and 15 percent by 2011.

Introduction

Mount Rainier in the Cascade Range of Washington State is drained by five major rivers: the Puyallup, Carbon, White, Nisqually, and Cowlitz Rivers (fig. 1). The Carbon and White Rivers are tributary to the Puyallup River, which, like the Nisqually River, drains to Puget Sound; the Cowlitz River is a tributary to the Columbia River, which forms the southwest boundary of Washington State. Large sediment loads in these river systems have resulted in high rates of aggradation in selected reaches, increasing channel migration and reducing flood-conveyance capacity (Beason and Kennard, 2007; Czuba and others, 2010). Multiple debris flows from Mount Rainier have delivered large volumes of sediment to these rivers, with most documented occurrences (between 1926 and 2006) in tributaries of the Nisqually River (Walder and Driedger, 1993; Walder and Driedger, 1994; Copeland, 2009). Much of the sediment delivered to the Nisqually River was transported downstream to Alder Lake, a reservoir that formed behind Alder Dam after its completion in 1945. Alder Lake has allowed for the quantification of sediment accumulation since 1945 from the Nisqually River, a river draining a glaciated stratovolcano, and the Little Nisqually River, a smaller river draining forested uplands of the Cascade Range (fig. 1).

Resource managers have few river-management options available that contend with large sediment loads, reduce flood risk, and do not adversely affect ecosystems (Czuba and others, 2010). Additionally, an apparent increase in the rate of aggradation along rivers within Mount Rainier National Park during the past two decades (Beason, 2007) may portend continued alluvial aggradation in lowland rivers as the sediment moves downstream. Resource managers responsible for the Puyallup and upper Nisqually River basins want to know the quantity of recently released alluvium and the historical trends of sediment transport so that they can begin to anticipate the timing and magnitude of the downstream movement of mobilized sediment. To assist with answering these questions, Pierce and King Counties requested that the U.S. Geological Survey (USGS) analyze the fluvial geomorphic response of rivers downstream of Mount Rainier, Washington.

The objectives of the overall study are to estimate sediment input from the upper basins of rivers draining Mount Rainier, and to estimate downstream transport of this sediment through the Puyallup River network (Puyallup, Carbon, and White Rivers) and the upper Nisqually River upstream of Alder Lake. This report addresses one component of the overall study: the estimation of the volumes of sediment deposited in Alder Lake between 1945 and 2011 from the Nisqually and Little Nisqually Rivers.

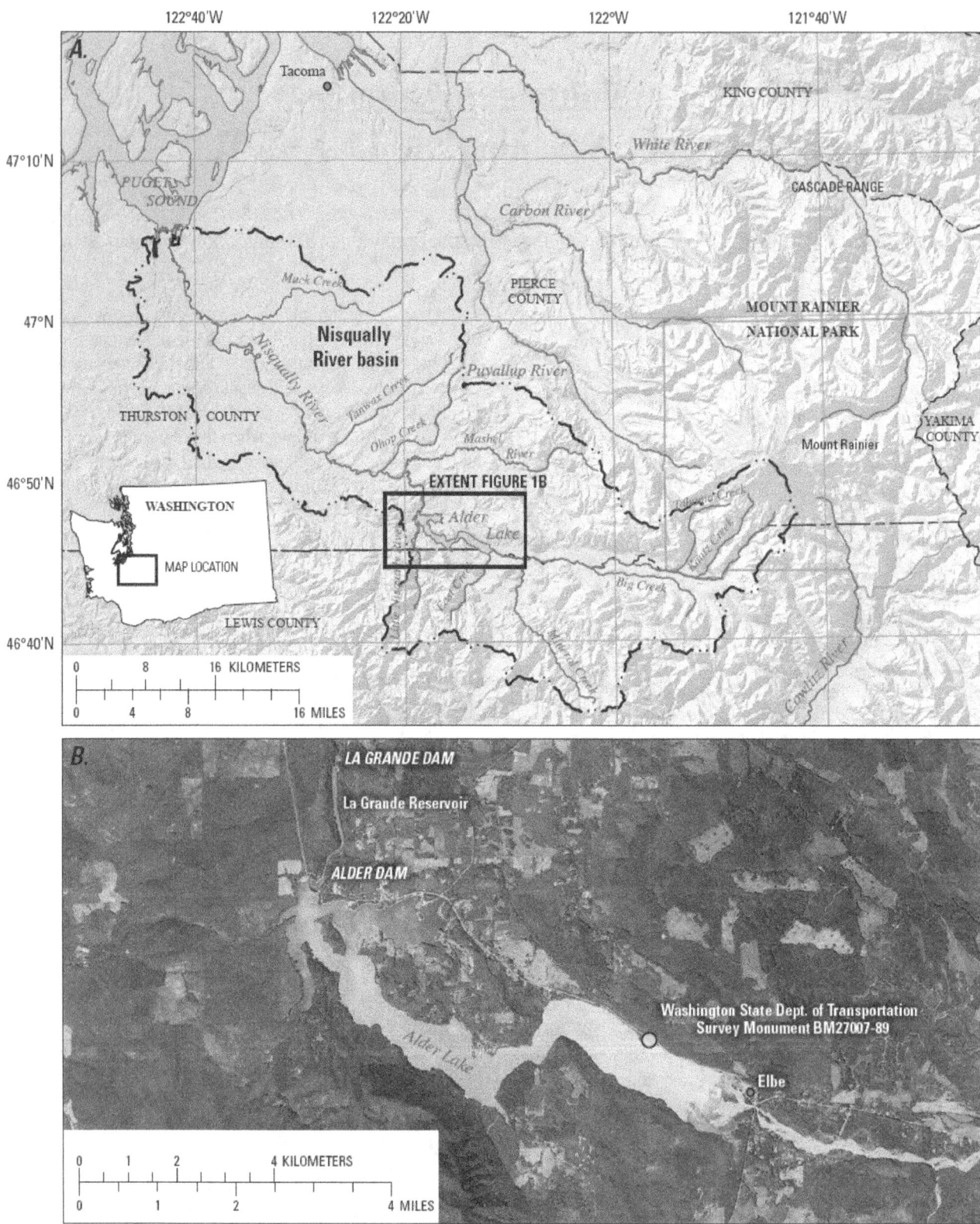

National Agricultural Imagery Program 2009, UTM zone 10, NAD83, 1 meter resolution.

Figure 1.   Location and extent of Alder Lake within the Nisqually River basin, Washington.

Purpose and Scope

This report documents changes in sediment volume in Alder Lake, Nisqually River basin, Washington, from 1945 to 2011. Estimates of the changes are based on comparisons of elevation surfaces for 1945, 1956, 1985, and 2011. The data sources were elevation-contour maps from surveys in 1945, 1956, and 1985 and from bathymetric data collected in Alder Lake on October 18–19, 2010, February 8, 2011, and April 19–20, 2011. These surfaces were then used to compute changes in sediment volume in Alder Lake since 1945. The volume change of the Nisqually River delta in Alder Lake was computed cumulatively from 1945 to 1956, 1985, and 2011 and also incrementally for 1945–56, 1956–85, and 1985–2011. The volume change of the Little Nisqually River delta in Alder Lake was computed for 1945–2011.

Description of Nisqually River Basin

The major tributaries (and associated basin areas) to Alder Lake (fig. 1) include the Nisqually River (approximately 590 square kilometers [km²]), the Little Nisqually River (approximately 67 km²), and East Creek (approximately 35 km²). The dominant land cover of all the basins upstream of Alder Lake is forest, but some tributaries also drain active glaciers on Mount Rainier. The source of the Nisqually River is on the southwestern slopes of Mount Rainier, a glaciated stratovolcano in the Cascade Range of western Washington with a summit elevation of approximately 4,393 meters (m). The total basin area of the Nisqually River is approximately 2,000 km² and the river drains to Puget Sound (fig. 1A). The major tributaries to the Nisqually River, also draining glaciers on Mount Rainier, include Kautz and Tahoma Creeks. Additional tributaries to the Nisqually River not draining glaciated terrain but entering the Nisqually River upstream of Alder Lake include Big and Mineral Creeks. East Creek and the Nisqually River enter Alder Lake at the eastern end of the lake, and both tributaries contribute sediment to the deltas that form at their adjacent mouths. The Little Nisqually River enters from a steep canyon into a southwestern arm of Alder Lake that joins the main lake near its outlet at Alder Dam (fig. 1B).

Alder Lake effectively traps most sediment delivered to it, reducing the amount of sediment delivered downstream. Just downstream of Alder Lake and Alder Dam is the smaller La Grande Reservoir and La Grande Dam, which was completed about the same time as Alder Dam (fig. 1B). Downstream of these dams, the major tributaries that enter the Nisqually River include the Mashel River, Ohop Creek, Tanwax Creek, and Muck Creek before the Nisqually River enters Puget Sound (fig. 1). The Nisqually River delta in Puget Sound is currently (2011) the site of the largest tidal marsh restoration project in the Pacific Northwest designed to assist in the recovery of Puget Sound salmon and wildlife populations (Nisqually Delta Restoration Partnership, 2011).

Understanding sediment delivery of the Nisqually River to Alder Lake can help fill a data gap for restoration-project managers planning for the future of the Nisqually River delta in Puget Sound.

In western Washington, periods of high streamflow occur during autumn and winter, coinciding with periods of maximum precipitation, and in spring or early summer, due to the seasonal rise in temperature and subsequent melting of snowpack at high elevations. In the western Cascade Range, orographic lifting of moisture-laden air masses brought in by frontal systems from the Pacific Ocean results in heavy precipitation, with annual precipitation ranging from 1.5 to 2.5 m (National Oceanic and Atmospheric Administration, 2011). The highest elevations of Mount Rainier remain snow covered through summer and have many large and expansive glaciers. Snowfall usually begins at high elevations in September and maximum snow depths usually are reached in early March (National Oceanic and Atmospheric Administration, 2011). Average winter snowfall ranges from 1.3 to 1.9 m at elevations of approximately 300 m, increasing to 10–15 m at elevations from 1,200 to 1,700 m (National Oceanic and Atmospheric Administration, 2011).

Brief History of Dams on the Nisqually River

In 1907, the city of Tacoma, Washington, was having trouble securing a reliable supply of electrical power. In 1909, its citizens voted to approve the construction of a hydroelectric power-generation plant on the Nisqually River (Malloy and Ott, 1993). The first Nisqually River hydroelectric project began with the construction of the La Grande Diversion Dam in February 1910, which was completed in August 1912. The first La Grande Dam was approximately 11-m high and 69-m wide (Malloy and Ott, 1993). In 1914, the town of Alder built the first Alder Dam at the confluence of Alder Creek and the Nisqually River, and used its reservoir as a mill pond (Johnstone and the South Pierce County Historical Society, 2011). Both dams were replaced in the second stage of the Nisqually River hydroelectric project by the current La Grande and Alder Dams (Tacoma Public Utilities, Tacoma Power, 2011). Construction began on the second Alder Dam in 1942 and was completed in 1945 (fig. 2; Johnstone and the South Pierce County Historical Society, 2011; Tacoma Public Utilities, Tacoma Power, 2011). The filling of Alder Lake began in January 1945 and electricity generation at Alder Dam began in September 1945 (Johnstone and the South Pierce County Historical Society, 2011). Alder Dam is a concrete arch dam approximately 101-m high and 490-m wide (fig. 3; Tacoma Public Utilities, Tacoma Power, 2011). La Grande Dam is a concrete gravity and embankment dam, constructed in 1945 approximately 3.2 kilometers (km) downstream of Alder Dam, and is approximately 66-m high and 220-m wide (Tacoma Public Utilities, Tacoma Power, 2011). Throughout the rest of this report, 'pre-dam' and 'post-dam' refer to the time prior to and after completion of the second Alder Dam in 1945, respectively.

Figure 2.   Construction of Alder Dam on the Nisqually River, Washington, July 20, 1943. (Courtesy of Tacoma Public Utilities, Tacoma Power.)

Figure 3. Alder Dam on the Nisqually River, Washington. (Courtesy of Tacoma Public Utilities, Tacoma Power, date unknown.)

Tacoma Power of Tacoma Public Utilities manages the water-surface elevation of Alder Lake with the primary goal of maintaining downstream river flows at or above a specified minimum. The secondary goal is to maintain a high lake elevation during prime recreation months. Alder Lake has little capacity to provide downstream flood control; however, when possible, Tacoma Power lowers the elevation of Alder Lake during winter months to enable some capture of high inflow rates from rainfall and snowmelt. The maximum water-surface elevation of Alder Lake, which is controlled by the dam spillway, is approximately 367 m, and the lowest allowable elevation, which is controlled by the water intake at the dam, is approximately 338 m (Tacoma Public Utilities, Tacoma Power, 2011).

Major Debris Flows from Mount Rainier in the Nisqually River Basin

Between 1926 and 2006, 51 debris flows have been documented within Mount Rainier National Park, 48 of which were located in tributaries of the Nisqually River (Walder and Driedger, 1993; Walder and Driedger, 1994; Copeland,

2009). However, this historical debris-flow record is likely incomplete because most events were documented only when they damaged park infrastructure or were large enough to be noticed. This historical record also is skewed toward the Nisqually River basin because this basin has the largest staff presence and is the most heavily visited in the park.

Debris flows are often triggered by heavy rainfall or glacial outburst flooding. Heavy rainfall on October 2–3, 1947, led to a series of four debris flows in Kautz Creek attributed to a combination of rain and glacial outburst flooding (Crandell, 1971; Walder and Driedger, 1993). The event mobilized about 40 million cubic meters (m^3) of sediment. Much of the fine-grained material was readily transported downstream and deposited in Alder Lake (Crandell, 1971). Debris flows were infrequently reported in Mount Rainier National Park between 1948 and 1966 (Copeland, 2009). From 1967 through 2006, at least 28 individual debris-flow events were recorded on Tahoma Creek (Walder and Driedger, 1994; Copeland, 2009). Although the historical record of observation is incomplete, there seems to be an increase in Mount Rainier debris-flow activity from the 1970s to 2006 (Walder and Driedger, 1993; Walder and Driedger, 1994; Copeland, 2009).

Methods

This study compared historical and modern elevation data to estimate volumes of sediment deposited in Alder Lake from its two major tributaries. This section describes how three historical elevation-contour maps of the Alder Lake area representing conditions in 1942–44, 1956–57, and 1985 were converted to digital format. This section also describes how an acoustic Doppler current profiler (ADCP) was used to measure bathymetry in Alder Lake in 2010–11. These data were used to generate elevation surfaces in a geographic information system (GIS) from which the net change in sediment volume in Alder Lake between pre- and post-dam conditions could be computed.

Description of Historical Contour Maps and Conversion to Digital Format

Historical elevation-contour maps were used to generate elevation surfaces for years 1945, 1956, and 1985. Tacoma Power provided the USGS with digital images of three historical paper elevation-contour maps of the Alder Lake area representing conditions in 1942–44, 1956–57 and 1985 (Jeff Singleton, Tacoma Public Utilities, Tacoma Power, written commun., 2010). The 1942–44 and 1956–57 contour maps were surveyed by Tacoma Power or one of its contractors, and the 1985 contour map was surveyed by the USGS. The exact methods used in these historical surveys are unknown, but information about survey dates, datums, and limited survey notes were recorded on the paper maps.

1945 Elevation-Contour Map

An elevation-contour map of the entire pre-dam Alder Lake area was represented on four separate map sheets. The dates of the map sheets spanned from September 1942 to October 1944 (September 26, 1942, November 10, 1942, November 20, 1942, and October 24, 1944), and were earliest near the proposed Alder Lake Dam site, and most recent near the mouth of the Nisqually River. The contours representing 1942–44 conditions were drawn at 5-ft intervals and were referenced to the Tacoma Power–Alder Lake project datum (vertical) in feet. It was assumed that negligible changes in elevation occurred between 1942 and 1945 at the location of the Nisqually and Little Nisqually River deltas in Alder Lake, and the composite elevation surface constructed from the historical map sheets are referred to in this report as the 1945 surface.

1956 Elevation-Contour Map

An elevation-contour map of the bed of Alder Lake near the mouth of the Nisqually River in Alder Lake, surveyed in 1956, was drawn on a copy of the October 24, 1944,

contour-map sheet to aid in the calculation (by Tacoma City Light, now Tacoma Power of Tacoma Public Utilities, dated June 15, 1956) of the change in sediment volume in the Nisqually River delta in Alder Lake. Additional contours were added to the map sheet on February 21, 1957, extending the 1956 contours from approximately 2.3 km to 2.9 km into the lake. The elevation contours representing 1956–57 conditions were drawn at 1-ft intervals and were referenced to the Tacoma Power–Alder Lake project datum (vertical) in feet. The elevation surface created from the 1956–57 contours is referred to in this report as the 1956 surface.

1985 Elevation-Contour Map

A third historical elevation-contour map obtained from Tacoma Power represented the entire bed of Alder Lake on three map sheets, dated October 29, 1985. The elevation contours on the map sheets were drawn mostly at 10-ft intervals, with a few contours drawn at 5-ft intervals near the mouth of the Nisqually River in Alder Lake. The contours were referenced to the National Geodetic Vertical Datum of 1929 (NGVD 29) in feet. The elevation surface created from these contours is referred to in this report as the 1985 surface.

Digital Conversion of Historical Contour Maps to Elevation Surfaces

The historical elevation maps were scanned and georeferenced horizontally to the North American Datum of 1927 (NAD 27) and projected into Universal Transverse Mercator zone 10 (UTM10) coordinates in units of meters. The digital maps were spatially registered in ArcGIS 9.3, using the 2.5-m resolution USGS 1:24,000 topographic quadrangle digital raster graphic (DRG) as a base layer. The exception is for the 1945 elevation-contour map near the Little Nisqually River, where the DRG georeferencing was not accurate compared to the 2009 aerial imagery from the National Agriculture Imagery Program (NAIP; U.S. Department of Agriculture, 2011) or the 2011 survey data. Instead this contour map was spatially registered to the shoreline of the 2009 NAIP imagery from August 3, 2009, which had an elevation of 362.8 m based on historical records of lake-surface elevation at Alder Dam (Toby Brewer, Tacoma Public Utilities, Tacoma Power, written commun., 2011). At least four ground control points were matched between the scanned maps and the DRGs and usually consisted of surveyed section corners, if available. Using the georeferencing tools in ArcGIS, each georeferenced map was rectified by resampling the data to a grid, with a cell size of about 1.0 m, by assigning the nearest-neighbor value to each grid cell. The root-mean-squared error of the ground control points was generally less than 10 m. Contour lines were then digitized from the rectified maps and attributed with contour elevations referenced to the vertical datum of the historical contours. The datums for all digitized historical contours were then converted to the North American Datum of 1983 (NAD 83) and the North American Vertical Datum of 1988 (NAVD 88) in meters. Conversion of the vertical datum of the historical contours to NAVD 88 in meters required three steps: the conversion from the Tacoma Power–Alder Lake project datum in feet to NGVD 29 in feet (subtract 7.42 ft), from NGVD 29 in feet to NAVD 88 in feet (add 3.484 ft; value obtained from near Alder Dam, National Geodetic Survey, 2003), and from NAVD 88 in feet to NAVD 88 in meters. Elevation surfaces were generated from the historical elevation contours using the Topo-to-Raster tool in ArcGIS.

Data Collection and Processing of 2011 Bathymetric Survey

Bathymetry of Alder Lake was surveyed on October 18–19, 2010, February 8, 2011, and April 19–20, 2011, using a 600-kHz ADCP and a real-time kinematic (RTK) global positioning system (GPS) that received real-time network corrections by mobile phone. The ADCP measured water depth with four transducers arranged in a Janus configuration oriented at 20 degrees from the vertical (Simpson, 2002). The RTK-GPS was mounted directly above the ADCP and was used to horizontally and vertically reference the ADCP water-depth measurements to real-world coordinates. Lake-bed elevations were computed by subtracting the water-depths measured by the ADCP from the water-surface elevations measured by the RTK-GPS. An elevation surface was generated from the combined elevation points using the Topo-to-Raster tool in ArcGIS; the final surface is referred to as the 2011 surface in this report.

All horizontal surveyed data were collected using the World Geodetic System of 1984 (WGS 84) ellipsoid reference surface and projected into NAD 83 UTM10 in meters and vertical data were collected referenced to NAVD 88 in feet. Geoid model GEOID03 (National Geodetic Survey, 2011) was used to convert GPS-derived heights above the ellipsoid to orthometric heights, or elevations above NAVD 88. All final surveyed data are in meters and use coordinates in the UTM10 projection referenced to NAD 83 and NAVD 88 datums.

Real-time corrections for the RTK-GPS were available from a network of base stations in the Washington State Reference Network and transmitted to the onboard GPS through a mobile-phone internet connection (Washington State Reference Network, 2011). Dual frequency Trimble R8 GPS receivers, Trimble Survey Controller, and Trimble GPS antennas were used for all GPS work. Quality control RTK-GPS measurements were made at a nearby Washington State Department of Transportation (WSDOT) survey monument BM27007-89 (fig. 1; Washington State Department of Transportation, 2011). The positional accuracy of the WSDOT monument was last updated on May 1, 2008, and had a reported horizontal and vertical accuracy of 0.02 m

and 0.01 m, respectively (Washington State Department of Transportation, 2011). Three quality-control measurements of this survey mark on days of the survey were all within 0.03 m horizontally and 0.05 m vertically.

Bathymetric data were collected using a combination of cross sections, winding paths, and longitudinal profiles. Water-depth measurements were collected in WinRiver2 ADCP data-processing software and imported into MatLab for further processing. Water-depth measurements from each of the four transducers were processed as individual lake-bed elevation points in the bathymetric dataset. Water-depth measurements were corrected in MatLab for transducer orientation and instrument pitch and roll using data from the compass and tilt sensor of the instrument. Water-depth measurements were compensated for changes in the speed of sound in water, associated with temperature, using the temperature sensor of the instrument located near the transducers.

Independent water-temperature measurements made periodically near the ADCP verified that the instrument was reading temperature within 0.5°C. No measurements were made of the temperature profile throughout the water column; therefore, ADCP water-depth measurements were not compensated for temperature variations with depth. A 5°C error in temperature throughout the entire water column would bias water-depth measurements by 2 percent (Mueller and Wagner, 2009). During the survey, measured surface-water temperatures ranged from approximately 4 to 14°C and measured water depths ranged from approximately 0.5 to 70 m. The presence of a thermocline, defined as a region of abruptly changing water temperature that separates cold deep water from warmer surface water, would bias measured water-depth measurements low, and therefore would bias computed lake-bed elevations high. Assuming the presence of an unmeasured thermocline during the survey that results in an average temperature throughout the water column of 4°C, the largest depth-measurement errors would be introduced where the measured surface-water temperatures were high and water depths were deep. Near the Nisqually and Little Nisqually River deltas, the combination of measured surface-water temperature and depth that would introduce the largest possible depth-measurement error due to the presence of a thermocline were a surface-water temperature of approximately 7°C and a depth of approximately 20 m that would bias measured water depths low and computed lake-bed elevations high by approximately 0.25 m. Similarly, away from the deltas in the deeper main body of the lake, the combination of measured surface-water temperature and depth that would introduce the largest possible depth-measurement error due to the presence of a thermocline were a surface-water temperature of approximately 9°C and a depth of approximately 70 m that would bias measured water depths low and computed lake-bed elevations high by approximately 1.4 m.

The 2011 bathymetric survey had a high spatial resolution near the Nisqually and Little Nisqually River deltas in Alder Lake, and away from these areas of interest, both the spatial resolution and vertical accuracy decreased. Given the accuracy of the RTK-GPS and ADCP instruments, the possible presence of a thermocline, and the sparse resolution of the dataset in some areas, the estimated uncertainty of the 2011 elevation surface is 0.3 m near the deltas and 2 m away from the deltas.

Computation of Change in Volume between Elevation Surfaces

Cumulative changes in the volume of the Nisqually River delta in Alder Lake were computed for the 1945–56, 1945–85, and 1945–2011 by subtracting the 1945 surface from each of the more recent surfaces. The volume change for the Little Nisqually River delta in Alder Lake was computed only for 1945–2011. The spatial extent of the volume-change computation depended on the overlapping areas of the two surfaces and was limited to just beyond the extent of the delta at that time. The volume-change computation generated an increase in volume where the 1956, 1985, and 2011 surfaces were higher than the 1945 surface, and a decrease where these surfaces were lower than the 1945 surface. The net change in volume was computed by subtracting the total

decrease in volume from the total increase. The rate of net change in volume was computed by dividing the net change in volume by the number of years between the two surveys. The incremental net change in volume between each survey (between 1945 and 1956, 1956 and 1985, and 1985 and 2011) was computed as the difference between net changes in volume since 1945.

The exact methods used for each historical survey are unknown; however, a measure of vertical uncertainty was estimated based on the contour interval of the historical survey. An uncertainty in the vertical elevations of each historical surface was assumed to be one-half of the contour interval of the contours used to generate that surface. The estimated uncertainty of the net change in volume was computed from the combined vertical uncertainties of the two surfaces being compared, calculated as the square root of the sum of the squares of the vertical uncertainty of each surface, and multiplied by the surface area of the computation.

Channel reworking or bank erosion was assumed to remove sediment from one location in the lake and deposit it in another location in the lake, resulting in no net change in sediment volume. Therefore, estimates of net change in volume (total increases minus total decreases in volumes) represent the net volume of sediment contributed by the respective rivers to Alder Lake.

Changes in Sediment Volume of the Nisqually River Delta in Alder Lake

The Nisqually River transports sediment with particle diameters that span a wide range of sizes: from cobble and gravel (with particle diameters as large as several centimeters) to clay (with particle diameters as small as a few micrometers). Before construction of the earliest dam on the Nisqually River in 1910, the Nisqually River transported sediment downstream of the Alder Lake area, with the largest particles breaking down to smaller sizes before reaching Puget Sound. The historical channel of the Nisqually River was apparent in the pre-dam (1945) surface of the Alder Lake area (fig. 4). Since the formation of Alder Lake in 1945, the transport of sediment by the Nisqually River downstream of the Alder Lake area decreased dramatically. A relatively large amount of sediment deposited in a delta within Alder Lake that had prograded as far as 6 km from the mouth of the Nisqually River as of 2011 (fig. 5). The delta front is indicated by the

sharp decline in elevation in a narrow section near the center of the lake (fig. 5). The coarsest sediment (cobble and gravel) would have deposited nearest the mouth of the Nisqually River in Alder Lake. The sediment composing the delta presumably grades to finer sediment (sand and silt) farther into the lake. The finest sediment (clay) presumably settles out in the main body of Alder Lake or passes through the intake structure of Alder Dam and is transported downstream. However, the transport and fate of specific sizes of sediment or the composition of sediment deposits were not assessed because the sizes of the sediment deposited in Alder Lake were not measured.

East Creek enters Alder Lake adjacent to the Nisqually River and also contributes sediment to the Nisqually River delta in Alder Lake. However, because the land cover in the East Creek basin is similar to the Little Nisqually River basin and is smaller in drainage area, it is assumed that its sediment contribution is minor and that most of the sediment in the Nisqually River delta in Alder Lake is attributed to the Nisqually River basin.

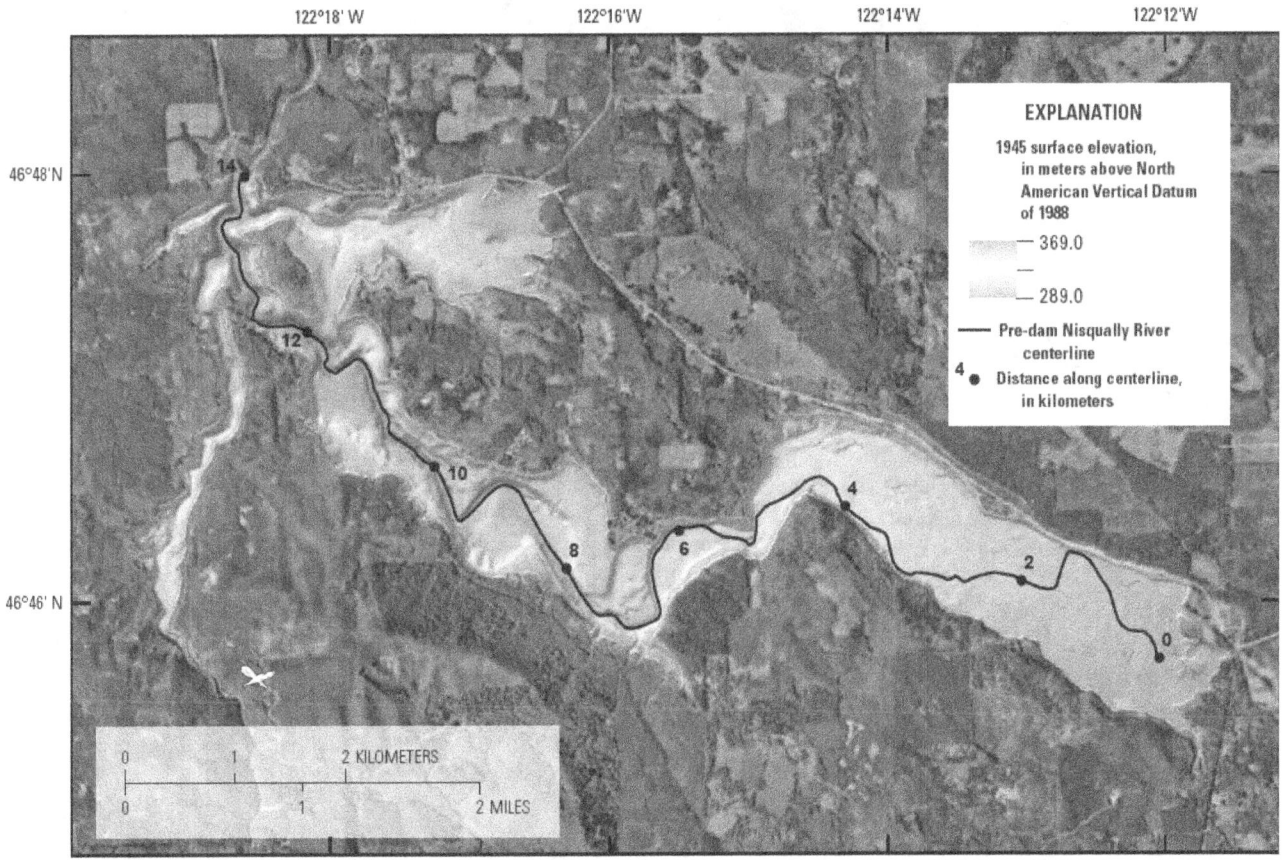

National Agricultural Imagery Program 2009, UTM zone 10, NAD83, 1 meter resolution.

Figure 4.   The 1945 (pre-dam) surface elevations of the Alder Lake area, Washington.

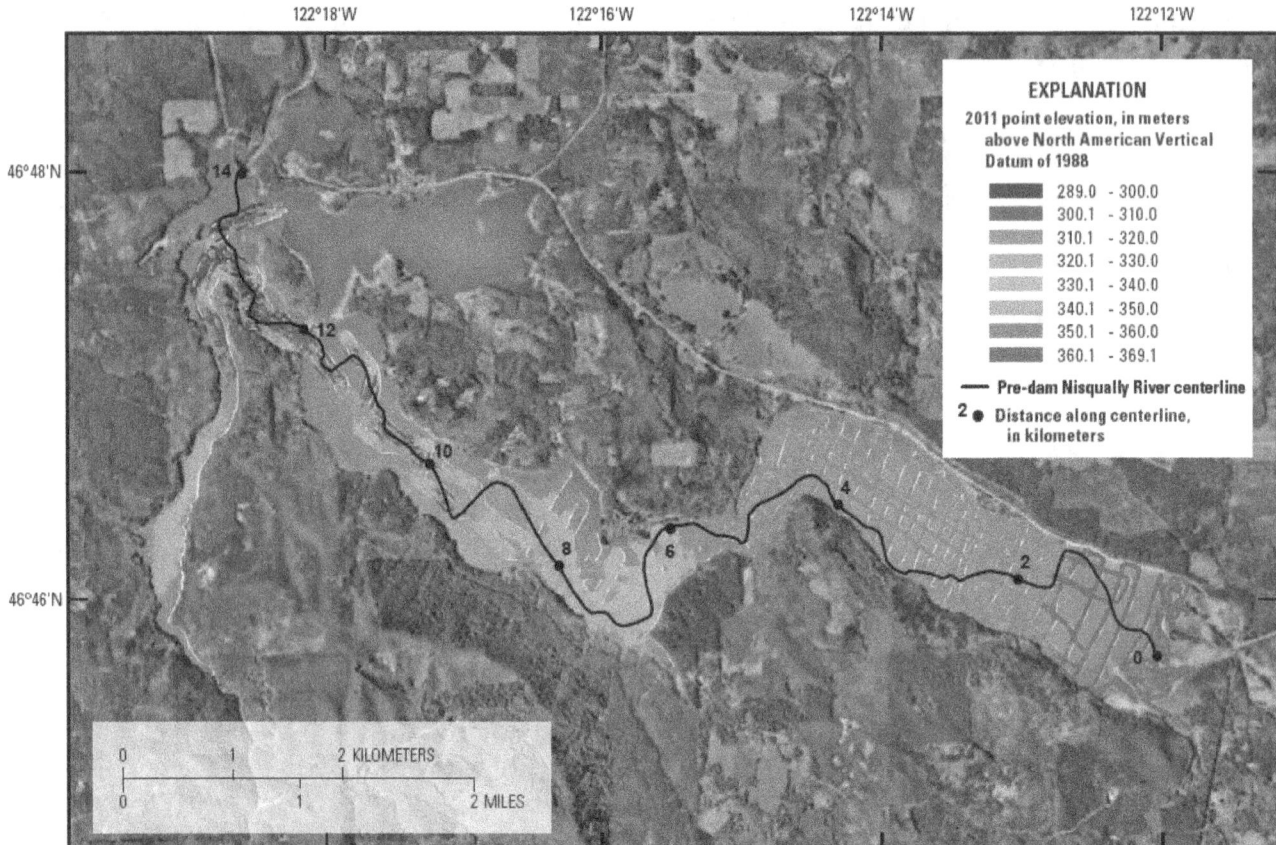

National Agricultural Imagery Program 2009, UTM zone 10, NAD83, 1 meter resolution.

Figure 5.   The 2011 point-elevation data of the bed of Alder Lake, Washington.

Comparison of elevation profiles along the historical channel of the Nisqually River for the 1945 (pre-dam) and 2011 surfaces showed the general change in elevation of the bed of Alder Lake between 1945 and 2011, with a maximum increase in the thickness of the delta deposit of approximately 30 m near its distal extent (fig. 6). Due to time limitations of the survey and the focus on the delta area, the 2011 elevation points (fig. 6) were sparse and uncertainty is larger close to the dam (between 8 and 14 km along the historical channel of the Nisqually River) than near the delta (between 0 and 8 km along the historical channel of the Nisqually River).

Because of differences in the resolution of the elevation contours, the four elevation surfaces of the Nisqually River delta region in Alder Lake show varying detail (fig. 7A-D).

The 1956 surface shows the most detailed features including a mound of sediment (fig. 7B, between 0 and 1 km along the approximate center of the delta) with distinct channel features cut into it. This mound of sediment has been attributed to sediment mobilized by the 1947 Kautz Creek debris flow (Crandell, 1971) that was transported from Kautz Creek downstream to the Nisqually River and deposited in Alder Lake. A photograph taken in 1956 (fig. 8) shows one of the channel features that was cut approximately 5 m down into the mound of sediment, which from the photograph appears to be composed of sand and finer-sized sediment. The exact location of the photograph is unknown, but based on comparable topographic features (fig. 8) and the 1956 surface (fig. 7B), the probable location is indicated in figure 7B.

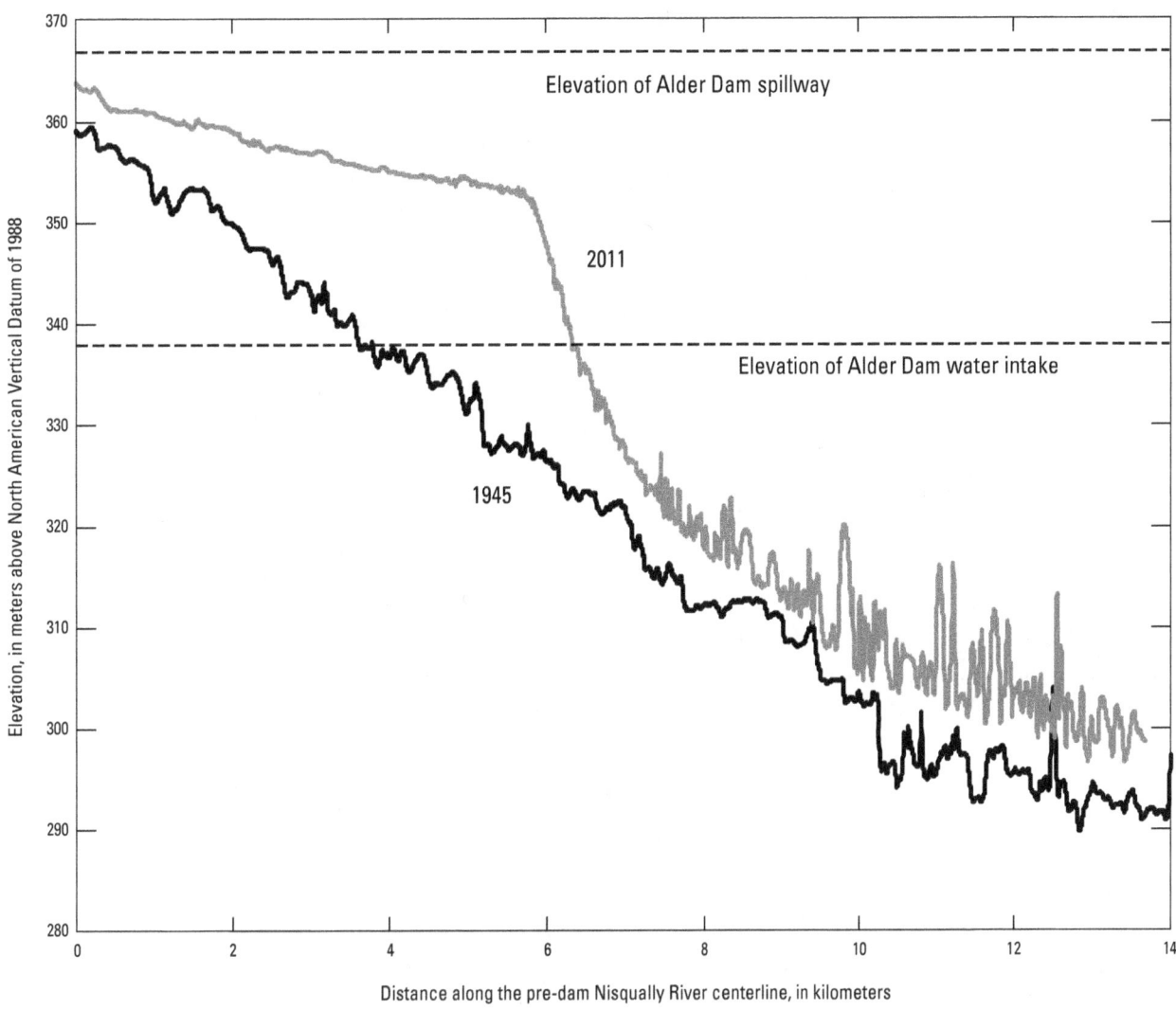

Figure 6. Elevation profiles along the pre-dam Nisqually River centerline for the 1945 (pre-dam) and 2011 surfaces of the bed of the Alder Lake, Washington. River centerline is shown in figures 4 and 5.

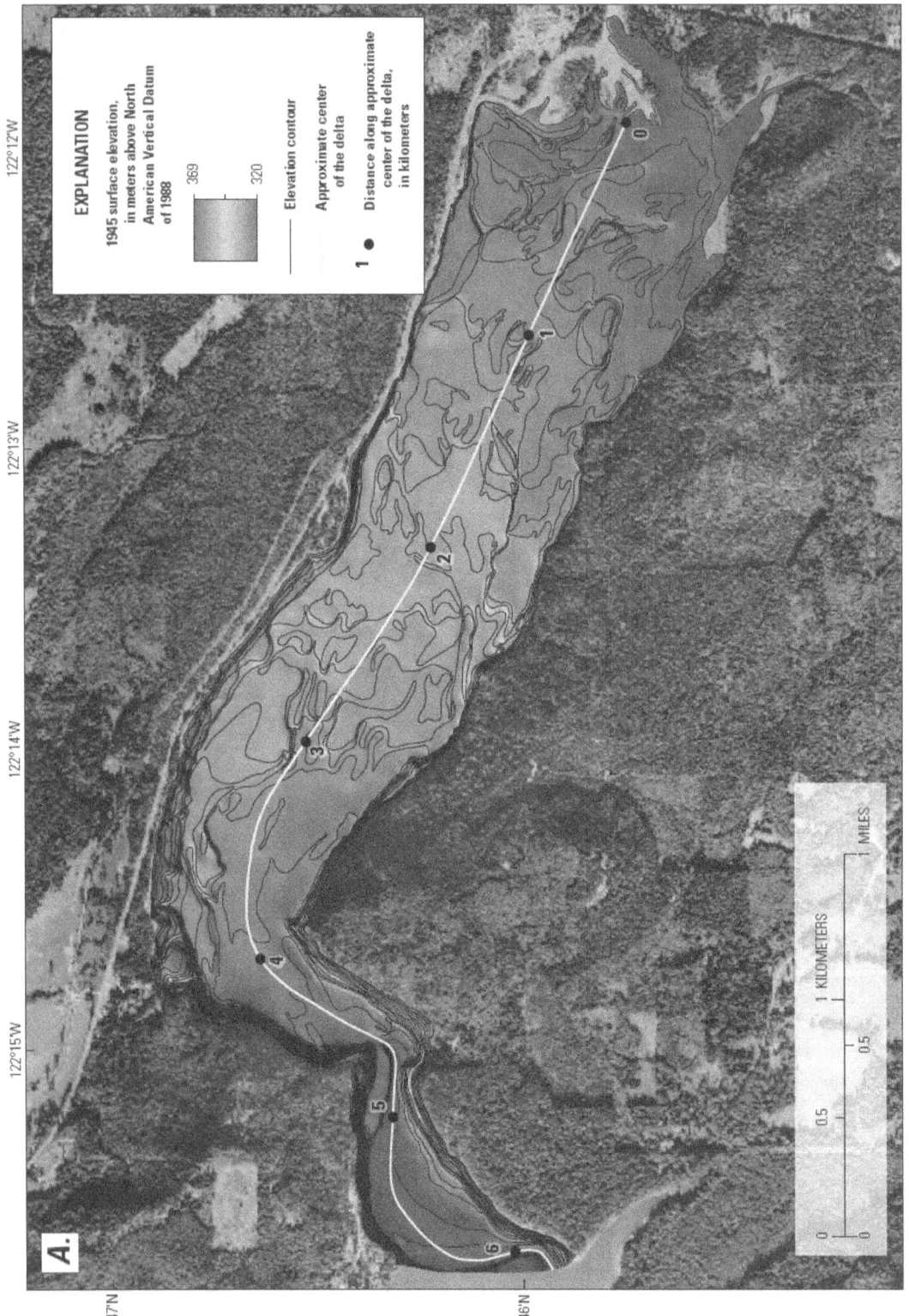

National Agricultural Imagery Program 2009, UTM zone 10, NAD83, 1 meter resolution.

Figure 7. Surface elevations of the Nisqually River delta in Alder Lake, Washington, from (*A*) 1945 (pre-dam; contours at 5-foot intervals); (*B*) 1956 (contours at 1-foot intervals; marker indicates the probable location of the photograph shown in figure 8); (*C*) 1985 (contours mostly at 10-foot intervals, with a few contours at 5-foot intervals); and (*D*) 2011.

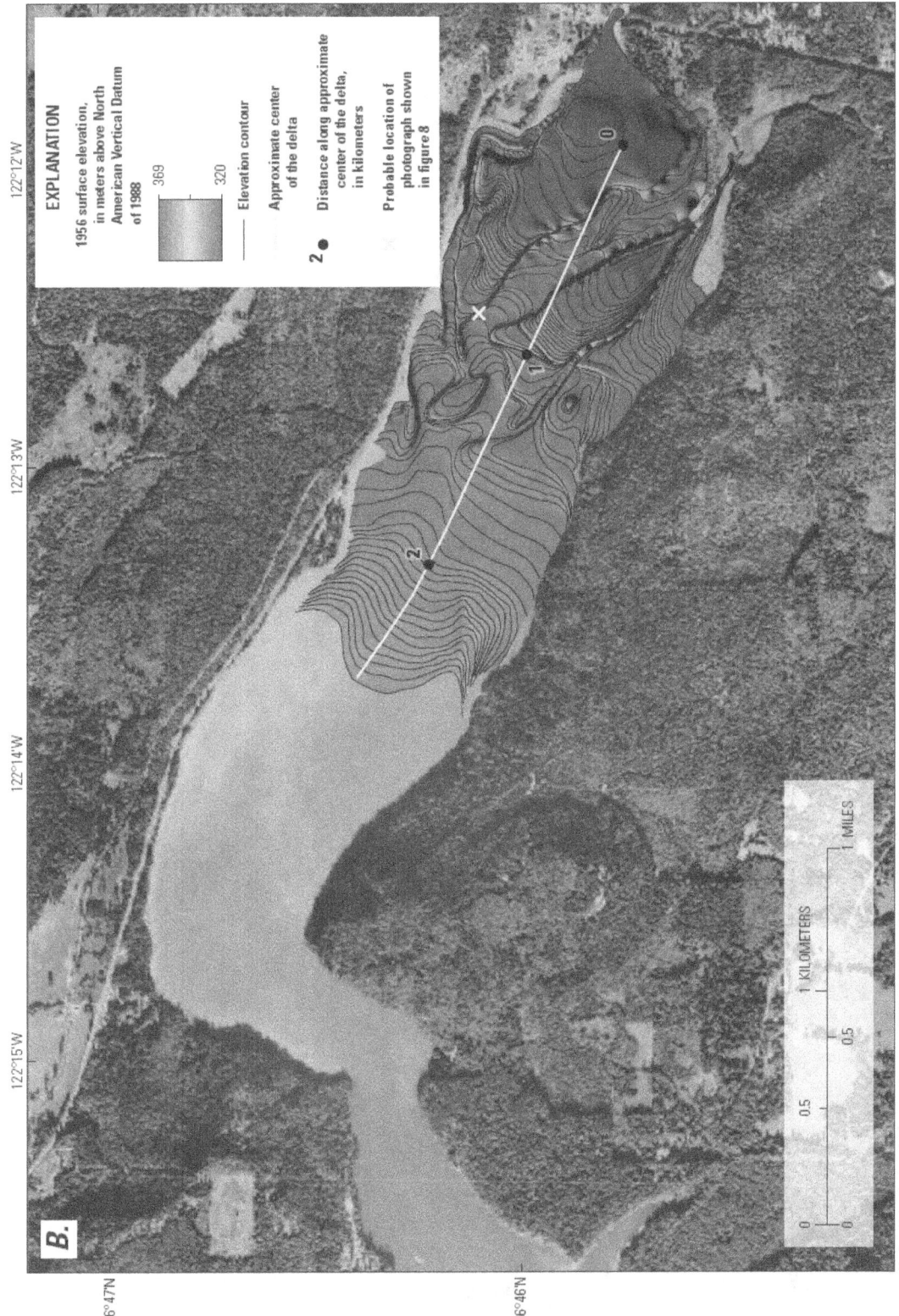

EXPLANATION

1956 surface elevation,
in meters above North
American Vertical Datum
of 1988

369

320

—— Elevation contour

—— Approximate center
of the delta

2● Distance along approximate
center of the delta,
in kilometers

☒ Probable location of
photograph shown
in figure 8

National Agricultural Imagery Program 2009, UTM zone 10, NAD83, 1 meter resolution.

Figure 7.   Continued.

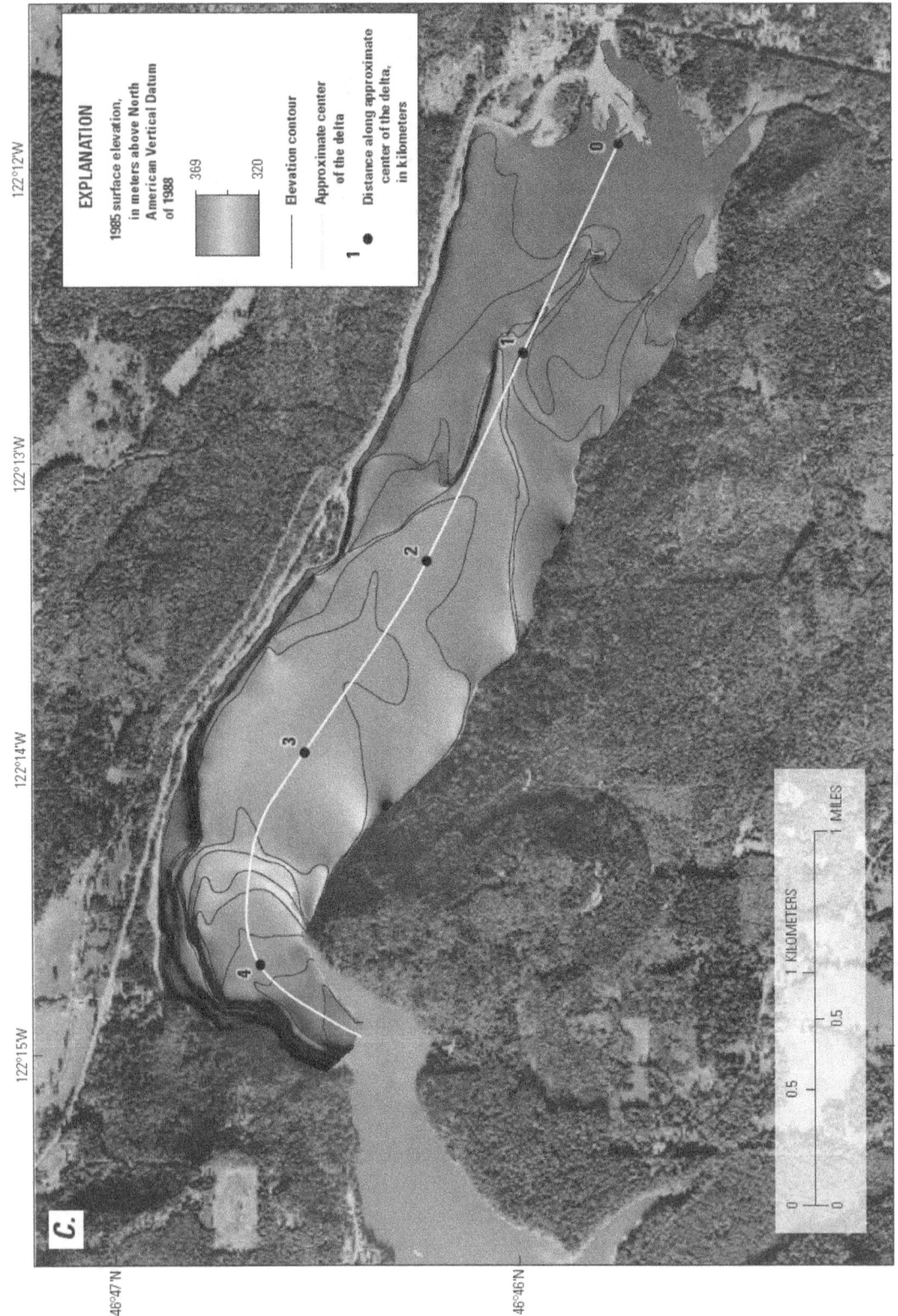

National Agricultural Imagery Program 2009, UTM zone 10, NAD83, 1 meter resolution.

Figure 7. Continued.

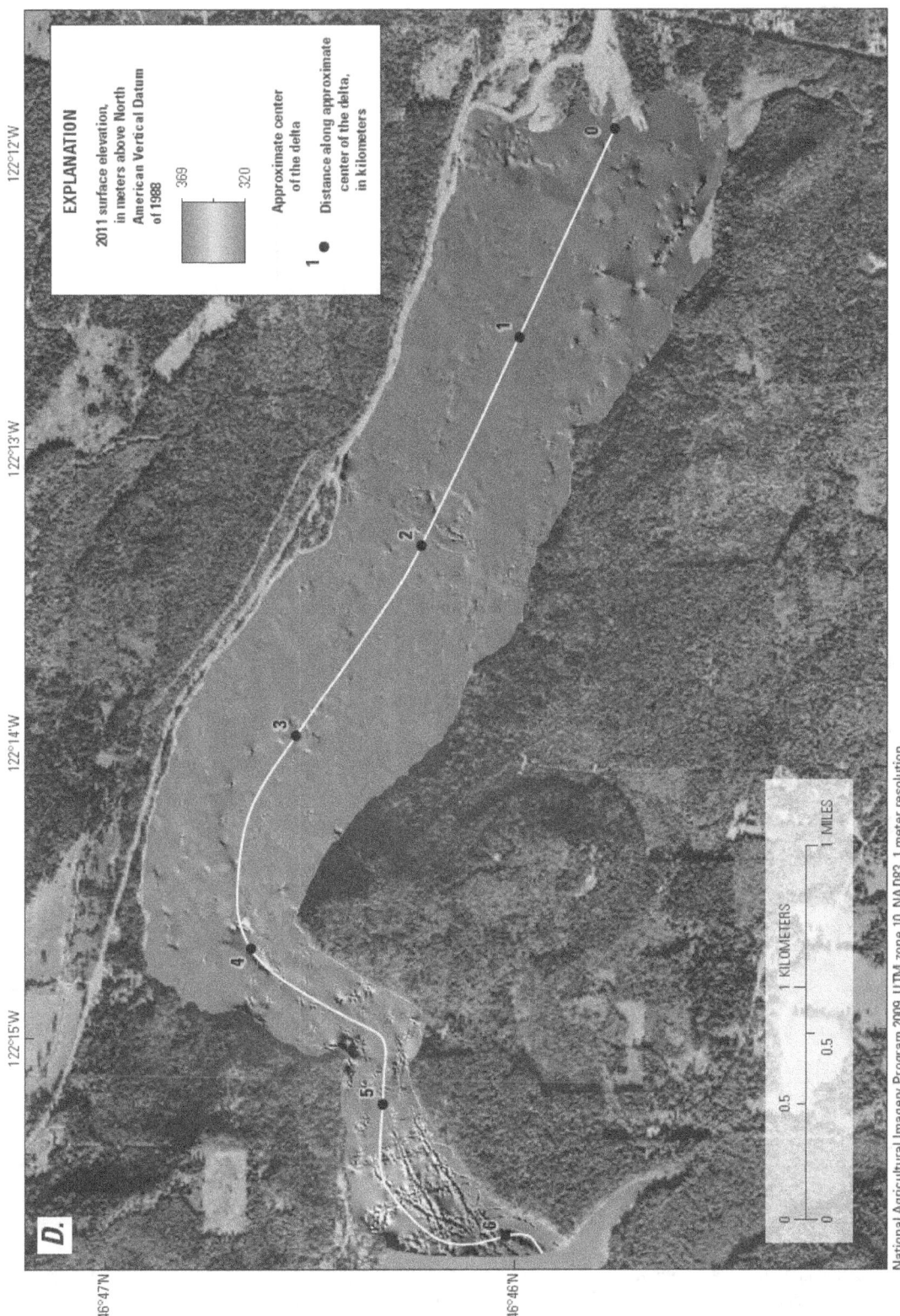

National Agricultural Imagery Program 2009, UTM zone 10, NAD83, 1 meter resolution.

Figure 7. Continued.

Figure 8.   Sediment deposited in Alder Lake near Elbe, Washington, March 28, 1956. The probable location of the photograph is indicated in figure 7B; view is looking southeast. (Courtesy of Tacoma Public Utilities, Tacoma Power.)

An elevation profile for these surfaces along a line through the approximate center of the Nisqually River delta in Alder Lake (which is different than the former river centerline shown in figures 4 and 5 and used for the elevation profile in figure 6) shows the temporal evolution of the Nisqually River delta in Alder Lake (fig. 9; line shown in fig. 7A-D). The 1956 surface, which includes the contour data that were added in 1957, does not capture the distal extent of the delta at that time, but indicates that it was at least approximately 2.5 km into Alder Lake from the mouth of the Nisqually River. By 1985, the delta front prograded a total distance of approximately 3.5 km. Between 1985 and 2011, the delta front prograded an additional distance of approximately 2 km farther into Alder Lake.

The spatial distribution of the changes in elevation between 1945 and 1956, 1985, and 2011 shows where increases and decreases in elevations are distributed in the Nisqually River delta region in Alder Lake (fig. 10A-C).

Areas with the largest increases in elevation are at the distal end of the prograding delta. Areas with noticeable decreases in elevation are along the banks of the lake and near the area where the Nisqually River and East Creek enter the lake (fig. 1). Significant decreases in elevation are likely due to reworking of deposited sediment by the migration of channels across the delta deposit during periods of low water in the lake, due to erosion of the banks along the shore of the lake, or an artifact of the horizontal misalignment of the surveys, in which the two georeferenced surfaces were not perfectly oriented to each other. The substantial decrease in elevation between 1945 and 1985 (fig. 10B) is most likely an artifact of horizontal misalignment of the 1985 surface. Significant decreases in elevation between 1945 and 2011 (fig. 10C) are limited to the banks of Alder Lake where wave action appears to have eroded the banks of the lake. Ongoing erosion of the southeast bank of Alder Lake near the center of the lake was observed on April 19, 2011 (fig. 11).

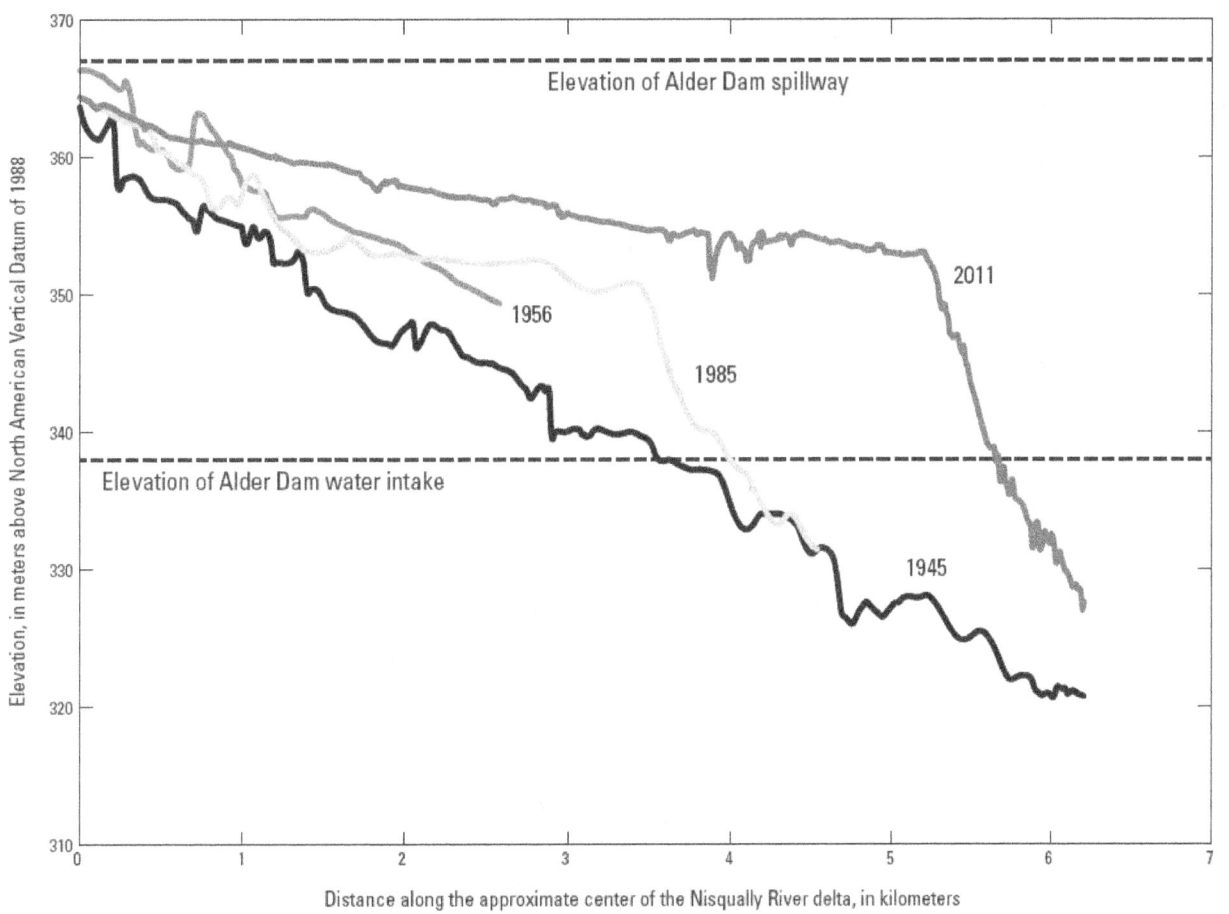

Figure 9.   Elevation profiles for the 1945 (pre-dam), 1956, 1985, and 2011 surfaces along a line through the approximate center of the Nisqually River delta in Alder Lake, Washington. (Line is shown in the maps in figure 7A-D).

National Agricultural Imagery Program 2009, UTM zone 10, NAD83, 1 meter resolution.

Figure 10.   Net change in elevation of the Nisqually River delta in Alder Lake, Washington, for (*A*) 1945–56, (*B*) 1945–85, and (*C*) 1945–2011.

National Agricultural Imagery Program 2009, UTM zone 10, NAD83, 1 meter resolution.

Figure 10. Continued.

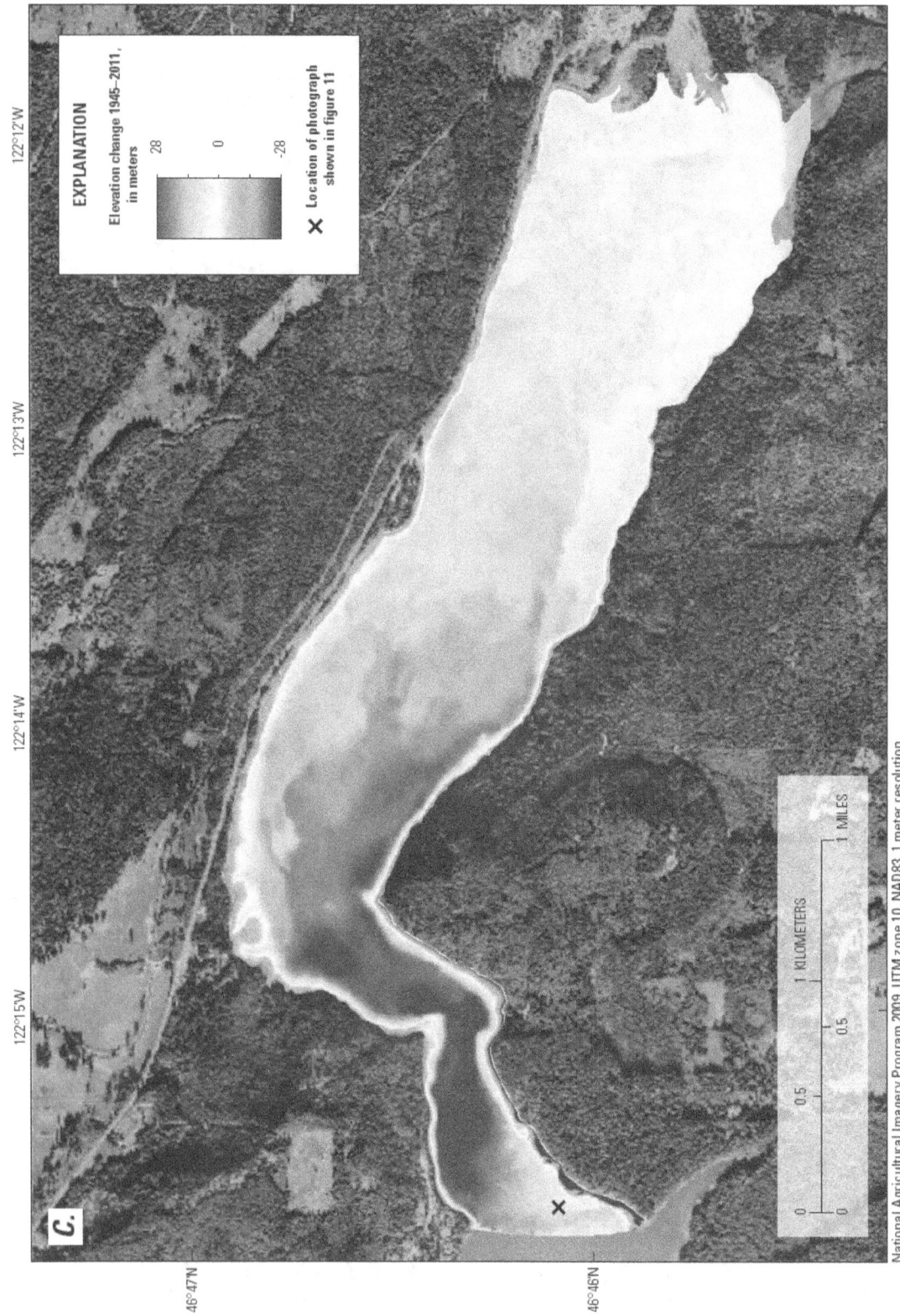

National Agricultural Imagery Program 2009, UTM zone 10, NAD83, 1 meter resolution.

Figure 10.   Continued.

Figure 11.   View looking south at the southeast bank of Alder Lake, Washington, near the center of the lake, April 19, 2011. (Location of the photograph is indicated in figure 10C. Photograph taken by Christiana Czuba, U.S. Geological Survey.)

The net change in volume and estimated uncertainty of the Nisqually River delta in Alder Lake between 1945 and 1956, 1945 and 1985, and 1945 and 2011 are 9 ± 2 million cubic meters, 22 ± 5 million cubic meters, and 42 ± 4 million cubic meters, respectively (table 1). The rate of net change in volume and estimated uncertainty for the Nisqually River delta in Alder Lake between 1945 and 2011 is $630,000 \pm 60,000$ m^3/yr. This is equivalent to a yield of $1,100 \pm 100$ (m^3/yr)/km^2 for the Nisqually River basin.

Tacoma City Light estimated that 7,215,000 m^3 of sediment accumulated in the Nisqually River delta in Alder Lake between 1944 and 1956. This estimate was cited by Mills (1976), but because this estimate did not include the additional contours that were added in February 1957, the estimated volume of sediment that accumulated in the Nisqually River delta in Alder Lake during that period was underestimated. The additional contours added in February 1957 in the volume calculation were used in this study to estimate the volume of sediment that accumulated in the Nisqually River delta in Alder Lake between 1945 and 1956 of 9,000,000 m^3 ($\pm$ 2,000,000 m^3; table 1). However, the contours added in 1957 did not fully extend to the distal extent of the Nisqually River delta in Alder Lake (fig. 9), and therefore, the estimate of the volume of sediment that accumulated in the Nisqually

River delta between 1945 and 1956, from this report, underrepresents the volume of sediment accumulated by 1956.

The 1947 Kautz Creek debris flow mobilized about 40 million cubic meters of sediment (Crandell, 1971). Some of this sediment deposited immediately in Kautz Creek, some deposited in the Nisqually River, and some transported to Alder Lake (fig. 7B and 8). Between 1945 and 1956, at least 9 million cubic meters of sediment had deposited in the Nisqually River delta in Alder Lake. The source of this sediment was from a combination of the background watershed contributions and from the 1947 Kautz Creek debris flow. Assuming that all of the 9 million cubic meters of sediment was from the Kautz Creek debris flow, then at most one-fourth of the sediment mobilized by the 1947 Kautz Creek debris flow deposited in Alder Lake by 1956.

The rates of incremental net change in volume between 1945 and 1956, 1956 and 1985, and 1985 and 2011 are 830,000, 430,000, and 770,000 m^3/yr, respectively (table 2). The largest rate of incremental net change in volume was for 1945–56. The rate of incremental net change in volume for 1956–85 was comparatively small, and may indicate that there was a shift in sediment delivery from Mount Rainier to the Nisqually River associated with a change in hydrologic conditions.

Table 1.   Net cumulative change in sediment volume of the Nisqually River delta in Alder Lake, Washington, and estimated uncertainty, 1945–56, 1945–85, and 1945–2011.

[**Abbreviations:** m², square meter; m³, cubic meter; m³/yr, cubic meter per year]

Period between surveys	Number of years between surveys	Surface area of volume computation (m²)	Total increase in volume (m³)	Total decrease in volume (m³)	Net change in volume (total increase minus total decrease) (m³)	Estimated uncertainty of net change in volume (m³)	Rate of net change in volume (m³/yr)	Estimated uncertainty of rate of net change in volume (m³/yr)
1945–56	11	2,500,000	9,300,000	100,000	9,000,000	2,000,000	830,000	180,000
1945–85	40	4,200,000	22,100,000	500,000	22,000,000	5,000,000	540,000	110,000
1945–2011	66	4,800,000	43,100,000	1,500,000	42,000,000	4,000,000	630,000	60,000

Table 2.   Incremental net change in sediment volume of the Nisqually River delta in Alder Lake, Washington, 1945–56, 1956–85, and 1985–2011.

[**Abbreviations:** m³, cubic meter; m³/yr, cubic meter per year]

Period between surveys	Number of years between surveys	Incremental net change in volume (m³)	Rate of incremental net change in volume (m³/yr)
1945–56	11	9,000,000	830,000
1956–85	29	12,000,000	430,000
1985–2011	26	20,000,000	770,000

Changes in Sediment Volume of the Little Nisqually River Delta in Alder Lake

The Little Nisqually River enters from a steep canyon into a southwestern arm of Alder Lake (fig. 1). The delta of the Little Nisqually River in Alder Lake is located where the lake widens as shown on the 1945 (pre-dam) and 2011 elevation surfaces (fig. 12). Elevation profiles along the historical channel of the Little Nisqually River from the pre-dam and 2011 surfaces indicate an increase in elevation of the bed of Alder Lake between 1945 and 2011, with a maximum increase of the delta deposit of approximately 10 m (fig. 13). Between 1945 and 2011, the Little Nisqually River delta in Alder Lake prograded less than 1 km into the lake (fig. 13) and did not

have as sharp of a break between the top and more steeply sloping front of its delta as did the Nisqually River delta in Alder Lake (fig. 6). The spatial distribution of the changes in elevation between 1945 and 2011 shows where increases and decreases in elevations are distributed in the Little Nisqually River delta region in Alder Lake (fig. 14). Areas with the largest increases in elevation are located toward the distal end of the prograding delta. Areas with noticeable decreases in elevation are located along the banks of the lake where there is a larger uncertainty between the elevation surfaces.

The net change in volume and estimated uncertainty of the Little Nisqually River delta in Alder Lake between 1945 and 2011 is 310,000 ± 110,000 m³ (table 3). The rate of net change in volume and estimated uncertainty for the Little Nisqually River delta in Alder Lake between 1945 and 2011 is 4,700 ± 1,600 m³/yr (table 3). This is equivalent to a yield of 70 ± 24 (m³/yr)/km² for the Little Nisqually River basin.

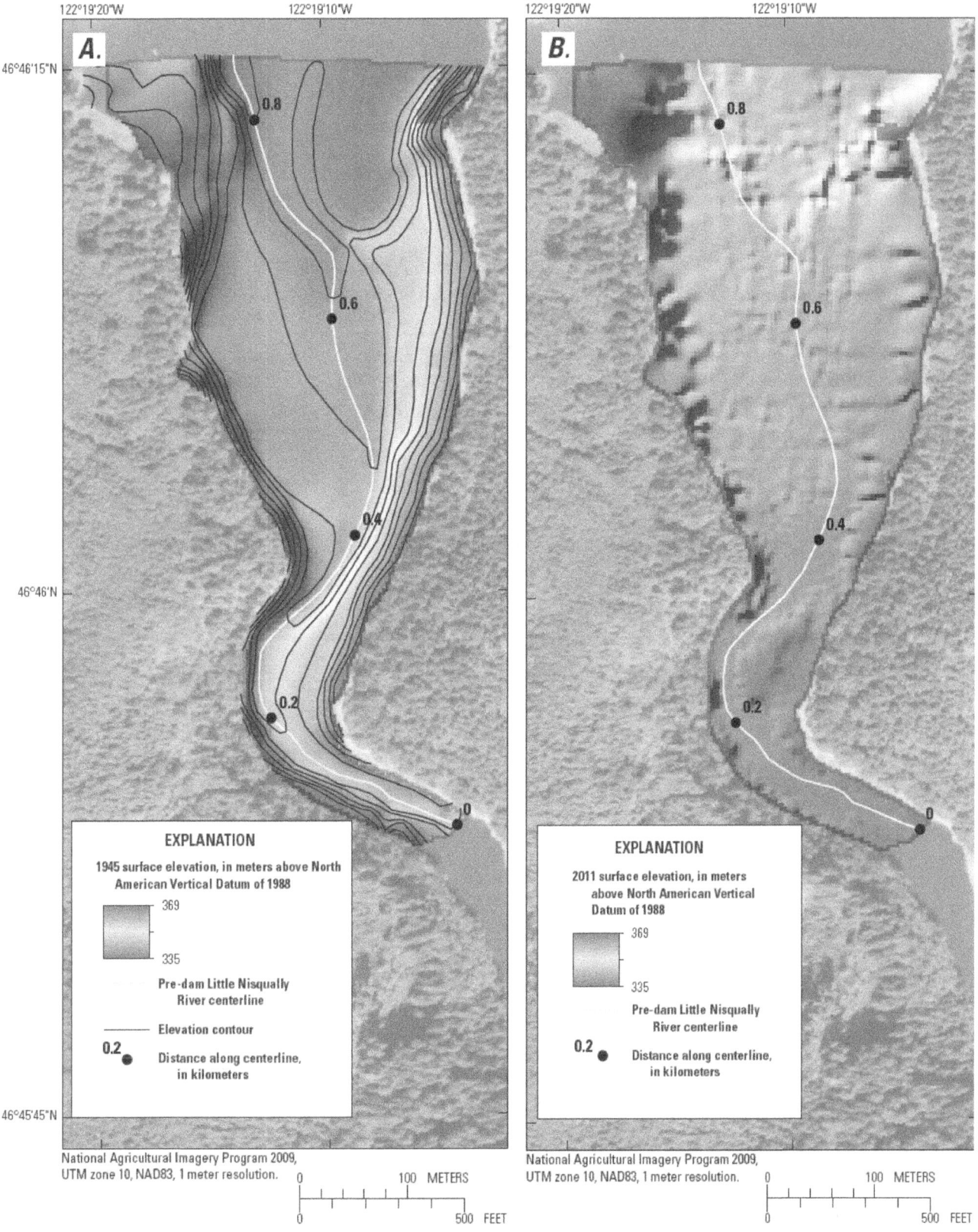

Figure 12. Spatial extent of the surfaces used to compute delta volume for the Little Nisqually River delta in Alder Lake, Washington, from (*A*) 1945 (pre-dam; contours at 5-foot intervals) and (*B*) 2011.

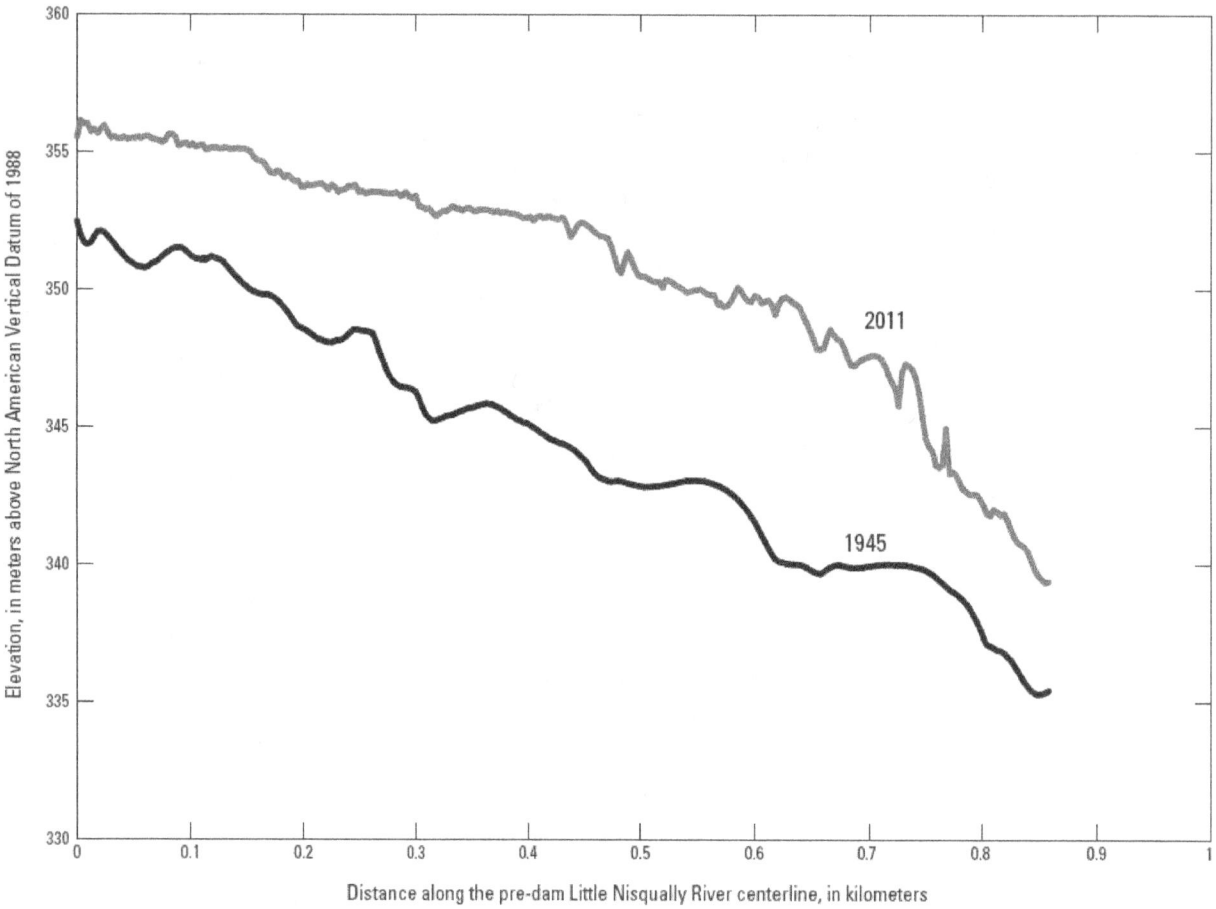

Figure 13.   Elevation profiles along the pre-dam Little Nisqually River centerline from 1945 (pre-dam) and 2011 surfaces of the Little Nisqually River delta in Alder Lake, Washington (shown in figures 12A–B).

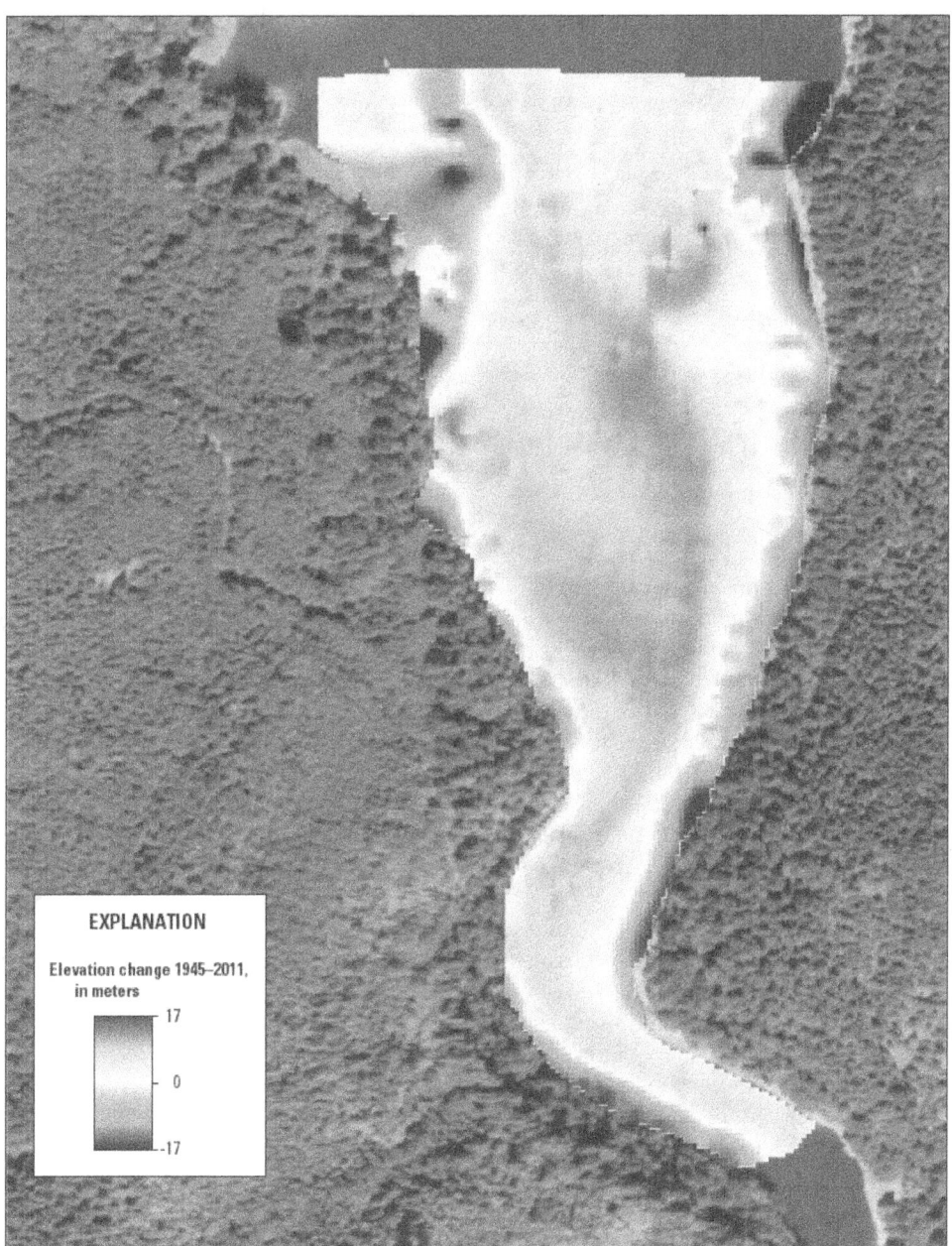

EXPLANATION

Elevation change 1945–2011, in meters

17

0

-17

National Agricultural Imagery Program 2009, UTM zone 10, NAD83, 1 meter resolution.

Figure 14.   Change in elevation of the Little Nisqually River delta in Alder Lake, Washington, 1945–2011.

Table 3.   Net change in sediment volume of the Little Nisqually River delta in Alder Lake, Washington, and estimated uncertainty, 1945–2011.

[**Abbreviations:** m^2, square meter; m^3, cubic meter; m^3/yr, cubic meter per year]

Period between surveys	Number of years between surveys	Surface area of volume computation (m^2)	Total increase in volume (m^3)	Total decrease in volume (m^3)	Net change in volume (total increase minus total decrease) (m^3)	Estimated uncertainty of net change in volume (m^3)	Rate of net change in volume (m^3/yr)	Estimated uncertainty of rate of net change in volume (m^3/yr)
1945–2011	66	130,000	470,000	160,000	310,000	110,000	4,700	1,600

Sediment Deposition in Alder Lake 1945–2011

Alder Lake allows the quantification of sediment deposited in the lake since 1945 from the Nisqually and Little Nisqually Rivers. The volumes of sediment measured in Alder Lake provide estimates of the sediment yield from subbasins with different land covers and geomorphic processes. The volume of sediment deposited in the main body of the lake, away from the deltas, between 1945 and 2011 was estimated from limited data collected in 2011 and combined with the delta volumes to provide an estimate of the total amount of sediment deposited in Alder Lake since 1945. The total amount of sediment deposited since 1945 has decreased the total capacity of Alder Lake.

The annual sediment yield of the Nisqually [1,100 ± 100 (m^3/yr)/km^2] and Little Nisqually River basins [70 ± 24 (m^3/yr)/km^2] provides an estimate of the yield of two basins with different land cover and geomorphic processes. These estimates suggest that a basin draining a glaciated stratovolcano yields approximately 15 times more sediment than a basin draining forested uplands in the Cascade Range. This finding is consistent with the finding of Czuba and others (2011) that the largest sediment loads in rivers draining to Puget Sound are carried by rivers with glaciated volcanoes in their headwaters.

Although this study primarily focused on sediment deposition in the deltas in Alder Lake, the limited data collected in 2011 in the main body of the lake provides an estimate of the volume of sediment deposition between 1945 and 2011. Away from the deltas and within the coverage of the 2011 bathymetric survey (fig. 5), the only area that showed a consistent change in elevation between 1945 and 2011 was along an approximately 40-m-wide corridor of the pre-dam Nisqually River that extended from the distal extent of the delta of the Nisqually River to Alder Dam. These data indicate that additional sediment has deposited in the main body of Alder Lake to an average thickness of approximately 7.5 m along a 40-m-wide corridor of the pre-dam Nisqually River, effectively filling the former river channel to an elevation similar to the surrounding valley (fig. 6; between 8 and 14 km along the historical channel of the Nisqually River). Between

1945 and 2011, a change in volume and estimated uncertainty of 2,000,000 ± 600,000 m^3 has occurred along the corridor of the pre-dam Nisqually River in the main body of Alder Lake. This change in volume corresponds to an annual rate and estimated uncertainty of 33,000 ± 9,000 m^3/yr. The source of this sediment is likely from the Nisqually River that either bypasses the delta and settles out in the main body of the lake, from the front of the delta that travels in turbidity currents along the channel of the pre-dam Nisqually River, or from filling in while the lake was forming.

Estimates of the volume of sediment deposited in Alder Lake between 1945 and 2011 were focused in three areas: (1) the Nisqually River delta, (2) the main body of Alder Lake, along a 40-m-wide corridor of the pre-dam Nisqually River, and (3) the Little Nisqually River delta. In each of these areas the net deposition over this 66 year period was 42,000,000 ± 4,000,000 m^3, 2,000,000 ± 600,000 m^3, and 310,000 ± 110,000 m^3, respectively (fig. 15). These volumes correspond to annual rates of accumulation of 630,000 ± 60,000 m^3/yr, 33,000 ± 9,000 m^3/yr, and 4,700 ± 1,600 m^3/yr, respectively. Given these rates, the Nisqually River accounts for approximately 99 percent of sediment deposited in Alder Lake (approximately 94 percent in the delta and approximately 5 percent in the main body of the lake) at an annual rate of 663,000 ± 61,000 m^3/yr, and the Little Nisqually River accounts for approximately 1 percent.

The maximum volumetric capacity of Alder Lake in 1945 at the elevation of the dam spillway (elevation of approximately 367 m) was approximately 287 million cubic meters. Based on the cumulative net change in sediment volume in the Nisqually River delta in Alder Lake (table 1), the total capacity of Alder Lake since 1945 decreased by about 3 percent by 1956, 8 percent by 1985, and 15 percent by 2011. The total capacity of Alder Lake may decrease by 50 percent by as early as 2175, based on the 1945-2011 sediment accumulation rate. However, this estimate assumes that the conditions during the last 66 years will be representative of future conditions. This may not be the case, given estimations of more intense precipitation (Salathé, 2006) and warmer temperatures in western Washington during the next century (Mote and Salathé, 2010) that likely would increase the production and delivery of sediment from Mount Rainier.

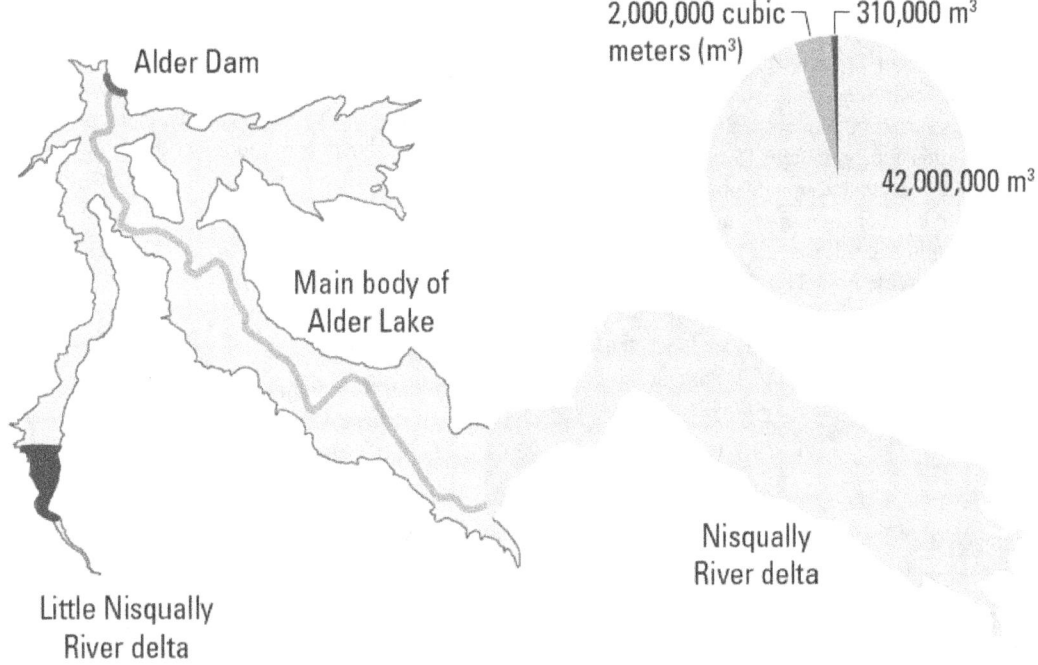

Figure 15. Volume of sediment deposition between 1945 and 2011 at three areas of Alder Lake, Washington: the Nisqually River delta; the main body of Alder Lake, along a 40-meter wide corridor of the pre-dam Nisqually River; and the Little Nisqually River delta.

Future Investigations

The 2011 bathymetric survey primarily focused on the Nisqually and Little Nisqually River deltas in Alder Lake to quantify the delivery of sediment by these rivers. A more detailed understanding of sediment delivery to Alder Lake and the fate of different sediment sizes within the lake would be possible with existing technology. For example, detailed features of the lake bottom could be resolved at sub-meter resolution using a multibeam echosounder. Depending on the amount of mixing between different layers of lake-bed sediment, it may be possible to obtain seasonal or yearly sediment deposition rates by coring the lake deposits at a number of locations within the deltas and a few beyond the distal extent of the deltas. The evolution of the lake deposits also could be determined from a structural map of the deposits that could be obtained through sub-bottom profiling using geophysical tools. Using a combination of the above methods, collection of physical sediment samples, and images of the lake bed, it would be possible to quantify the transport and fate of specific sizes of sediment and the composition of sediment deposits in Alder Lake.

Summary

The Nisqually River drains the southwest slopes of Mount Rainier, a glaciated stratovolcano in the Cascade Range of western Washington. The Nisqually River was impounded behind Alder Dam in 1945, forming Alder Lake. In this study, four digital elevation surfaces were generated from historical contour maps from 1945, 1956, 1985, and from a 2011 bathymetric survey of Alder Lake using an acoustic Doppler current profiler. These surfaces were then used to compute changes in sediment volume in Alder Lake since 1945.

The presence of Alder Lake allows the quantification of sediment deposited in the lake since 1945 from the Nisqually and Little Nisqually Rivers. Estimates of the volume of sediment deposited in Alder Lake between 1945 and 2011 were focused in three areas: (1) the Nisqually River delta, (2) the main body of Alder Lake, along a 40-m-wide corridor of the pre-dam Nisqually River, and (3) the Little Nisqually River delta. In each of these areas the net deposition over this 66 year period was 42,000,000 ± 4,000,000 m^3, 2,000,000 + 600,000 m^3, and 310,000 ± 110,000 m^3, respectively.

These volumes correspond to annual rates of accumulation of 630,000 ± 60,000 m^3/yr, 33,000 ± 9,000 m^3/yr, and 4,700 ± 1,600 m^3/yr, respectively. The annual sediment yield of the Nisqually [1,100 ± 100 (m^3/yr)/km^2] and Little Nisqually River basins [70 ± 24 (m^3/yr)/km^2] provides insight into the yield of two basins with different land cover and geomorphic processes. These estimates suggest that a basin draining a glaciated stratovolcano yields approximately 15 times more sediment than a basin draining forested uplands in the Cascade Range. Given the cumulative net change in sediment volume in the Nisqually River delta in Alder Lake, the total capacity of Alder Lake since 1945 decreased by about 3 percent by 1956, 8 percent by 1985, and 15 percent by 2011. Given the rate of sediment deposition for 1945-2011 in Alder Lake, the total capacity of Alder Lake may decrease by 50 percent by 2175, assuming the conditions during the last 66 years will be representative of future conditions.

Acknowledgments

We thank Tacoma Public Utilities, Tacoma Power for providing historical elevation-contour maps of the bed of Alder Lake and historical photographs, and James Foreman and Greg Justin, U.S. Geological Survey, for assistance with field surveys.

References Cited

Beason, S.R., 2007, The environmental implications of aggradation in major braided rivers at Mount Rainier National Park, Washington: Cedar Falls, Iowa, University of Northern Iowa, M.S. thesis, 165 p.

Beason, S.R., and Kennard, P.M., 2007, Environmental and ecological implications of aggradation in braided rivers at Mount Rainier National Park, *in* Selleck, J., ed., Natural Resource Year in Review—2006: Denver, Colo., National Park Service Publication D-1859, p. 52–53.

Copeland, E.A., 2009, Recent periglacial debris flows from Mount Rainier, Washington: Corvallis, Oreg., Oregon State University, M.S. thesis, 124 p.

Crandell, D.R., 1971, Postglacial lahars from Mount Rainier Volcano, Washington: U.S. Geological Survey Professional Paper 677, 75 p. (Also available at http://pubs.er.usgs.gov/publication/pp677.)

Czuba, J.A., Czuba, C.R., Magirl, C.S., and Voss, F.D., 2010, Channel-conveyance capacity, channel change, and sediment transport in the lower Puyallup, White, and Carbon Rivers, western Washington: U.S. Geological Survey Scientific Investigations Report 2010-5240, 104 p. (Also available at http://pubs.er.usgs.gov/publication/sir20105240.)

Czuba, J.A., Magirl, C.S., Czuba, C.R., Grossman, E.E., Curran, C.A., Gendaszek, A.S., and Dinicola, R.S., 2011, Sediment load from major rivers into Puget Sound and its adjacent waters: U.S. Geological Survey Fact Sheet 2011-3083, 4 p. (Also available at http://pubs.er.usgs.gov/publication/fs20113083.)

Johnstone, D.M., and the South Pierce County Historical Society, 2011, Upper Nisqually Valley: Arcadia Publishing, Charleston, South Carolina, 127 p.

Malloy, D., and Ott, J.S., 1993, The Tacoma Public Utilities Story, The First 100 Years: 1893–1993: Tacoma Public Utilities, Tacoma, Washington, 286 p.

Mills, H.H., 1976, Estimated erosion rates on Mount Rainier, Washington: Geology, v. 4, no. 7, p. 401-406.

Mote, P.W., and E.P. Salathé, 2010, Future climate in the Pacific Northwest: Climatic Change, v. 102, no. 1–2, p. 29–50.

Mueller, D.S., and Wagner, C.R., 2009, Measuring discharge with acoustic Doppler current profilers from a moving boat: U.S. Geological Survey Techniques and Methods 3A-22, 72 p.

National Geodetic Survey, 2003, VERTCON, version 2.1: National Geodetic Survey website accessed July 7, 2011, at http://www.ngs.noaa.gov/PC_PROD/VERTCON/.

National Geodetic Survey, 2011, GEOID03: National Geodetic Survey website accessed September 30, 2011, at http://www.ngs.noaa.gov/GEOID/GEOID03/.

National Oceanic and Atmospheric Administration, 2011, Climate of Washington: Western Regional Climate Center website accessed October 5, 2011, at http://www.wrcc.dri.edu/narratives/WASHINGTON htm.

Nisqually Delta Restoration Partnership, 2011, Nisqually Delta Restoration: Nisqually Delta Restoration Partnership website accessed October 5, 2011, at http://www.nisquallydeltarestoration.org/.

Salathé, E.P., 2006, Influences of a shift in North Pacific storm tracks on western North American precipitation under global warming: Geophysical Research Letters, v. 33, L19820, 4 p.

Simpson, M.R., 2002, Discharge measurements using a broadband acoustic Doppler current profiler: U.S. Geological Survey Open-File Report 2001-1, 123 p. (Also available at http://pubs.er.usgs.gov/publication/ofr011.)

Tacoma Public Utilities, Tacoma Power, 2011, Nisqually River Project—Hydro Power: Tacoma Public Utilities website, accessed October 7, 2011, at http://www.mytpu.org/tacomapower/power-system/hydro-power/nisqually-river-project/Default htm.

U.S. Department of Agriculture, 2011, National Agricultural Imagery Program: U.S. Department of Agriculture website, accessed October 6, 2011, at http://www.fsa.usda.gov/FSA/apfoapp?area=home&subject=prog&topic=nai.

Walder, J.S., and Driedger, C.L., 1993, Glacier-generated debris flows at Mount Rainier: U.S. Geological Survey Open-File Report 93-124. (Also available at http://pubs.er.usgs.gov/publication/ofr93124.)

Walder, J.S., and Driedger, C.L., 1994, Rapid geomorphic change caused by glacial outburst floods and debris flows along Tahoma Creek, Mount Rainier, Washington, U.S.A.: Arctic and Alpine Research, v. 26, no. 4, p. 319–327.

Washington State Department of Transportation, 2011, Geographic Services Survey Information System—BM27007-89: Washington State Department of Transportation website, accessed September 28, 2011, at http://www.wsdot.wa.gov/monument/report.aspx?monumentid=6370.

Washington State Reference Network, 2011, A regional cooperative of real-time GPS networks: Washington State Reference Network website, accessed March 15, 2012, at http://www.wsrn2.org/.

www.ingramcontent.com/pod-product-compliance
Lightning Source LLC
Chambersburg PA
CBHW080353290526

45791CB00009BA/2855